Facing the Future

Poems by Loman Bell

Copyright 2010 by Loman Bell. All rights reserved.

The credit for this book mainly, goes to the Bible and it's inspirational words of truth and faith. Pictures were either my photographs or some paintings I've done

To contact the author to order additional copies of this book or his other books and music:
Loman Bell
RR 4
Murray River, PE, C0A 1W0, Canada
lombell@yahoo.ca

His books are also available through www.amazon.com

Printing and binding by:
Lightning Source Inc. (US)
1246 Heil Quaker Blvd.
La Vergne, TN 37086 USA
Voice: (615 213-5815
Fax: (615) 213-4725
Email: inquiry@lightningsource.com
www.lightningsource.com

A *Southern Kings Arts Council* grant aided in the production of this book.

ISBN: 978-0-9866065-1-9

Dedication

I would like to dedicate this book to my God—the Lord God Jehovah, Jesus Christ His Son and the Holy Spirit. He has always been a real intricate part of my life.

Ever since I accepted God's Son, Jesus Christ as my Lord and my Saviour there's always been His wonderful kind presence in my life, like a good father or a Shepherd.

The big impact in all my life was having God to save, guide, and keep me day by day, there would be no other who could ever take his place.

Everything I do will be thanks to God for all the truth and help He's been to me.

Dear God I praise you and thank You for Your love and help and I'll dedicate this book as I have dedicated all my life, to You.

Loman Bell

Introduction

I have a personal relationship with Jesus, God's Son, and I have the joy of having Him with me day by day, and sharing those experiences with others. From my own encounters through life, with Jesus it's a real journey. I want to share some of my feelings about that.

One of my desires from these writings is to inspire soul searching and investigation. The main manuscript for background information is the Bible.

I believe if you take a real honest look you will find "The Bible" as old as time and as new as now—the Bible covers a time span from eternity to eternity.

This is just some of the ground I'm trying to cover through the material written here.

Loman Bell

ALWAYS DREAM

May you be in all life's scenes,
Always remembered by your dreams.
On each and every page in time,
Through every step you've done just fine.

Some days dark and dreary are,
Wake each morning to stay on par.
Don't let the rain discourage you,
Face each day with new hope true.

Keep your thoughts in there place,
Give your troubles to God by grace.
Journey here but never alone,
He knows and will welcome you home.

In your growing day by day,
Keep seeking truth all the way,
Leave doubts by the side of the road,
As you go on to heavens abode.

Climb those mountains; scale the heights,
Through the day, and in the night.
There is some danger, so be aware,
But don't fear with the light you bear.

Be friends for now and for always,
The lost need help through the maze.
Seek truth and keep going on,
When darkness fades, here comes the dawn.

Be prepared for eternity,
Everyone born must go and see.
God's love is present in everything,
He will always make us sing.

FACING THE FUTURE

DEDICATION IV

INTRODUCTION VI
    ALWAYS DREAM VII

MORNING POEMS 1
    HOUSE OF POEMS 2
    SOMETIMES IT FEELS STRANGE 3
    CIRCLES OF LIFE 4
    WE'VE LIVED, WE'VE LOVED LIFE 5
    THE FURY DOES BLAST 7
    NIGHT TIME JOY 8
    OUR ETERNAL HOME 9
    POOLS, STREAMS, AND RIVERS 11
    TOO MANY TROUBLES 13
    THE MIND OF GOD 15

ANGELS 17
    IN JESUS' HEART 18
    WITH THE ANGELS 19
    WHY CAN'T IT ALL BE TRUE? 20

DAY BY DAY 23
    A LIFE FULL OF MOUNTAINS 24
    ANOTHER TURN IN LIFE'S ROAD 25
    A THORN IN THE FLESH 26
    BEFORE THE RIVER 27
    CALLING HIS CHILDREN 28
    DELIVERANCE 29
    DO I STILL NEED MORE? 30
    DREAMING OF HEAVEN 31
    ETERNITY 32
    FAMILY BLESSINGS 33
    FORGIVING 34
    GETTING READY TO GO 35
    HAPPY NEW YEAR DECLARATION 36
    HAVE YOU KNOWN FEAR? 37
    HE DIED FROM A BROKEN HEART 38
    I WANT TO SERVE MY LORD 39
    IF YOU CROSS THE RIVER 40
    JUST UP ON THE HILL ON THE OTHER SIDE ... 41
    LIFE IS A MIRACLE 42
    LIFE TO LIVE OVER AGAIN 43

TABLE OF CONTENTS

- LOVE 44
- LOVE IS THE ONLY ANSWER 45
- MELODY OF LIFE 47
- MAN AND CREATION 48
- PANIC OR PEACE 49
- POOR AND NEEDY 50
- RISE AND SHINE 51
- SEARCHING, SEARCHING 52
- THE CRIMSON VALLEY 53
- THE SUNSHINE IS YOURS AND MINE 54
- THERE IS STILL HOPE 55
- THEY CAME TO CHURCH WITH DADDY ONE MORE TIME 56
- THROUGH TROUBLED WATERS 57
- TRY AND TRY 58
- WHERE IS HEAVEN? 59
- WORKING FOR JESUS 60

JESUS SECTION 61
- JESUS CARES 62
- JESUS CLIMBED THAT MOUNTAIN 63
- JESUS DIED FOR ALL 64
- JESUS IS ON MY SIDE 65
- JESUS OUR EXAMPLE 66
- JESUS' PRESENCE 67
- THE VINE 68
- JESUS WALKED ON THE WATER 69
- YES VICTORY 70

DEATH AND RESURRECTION 71
- BETRAYED TO CLAIM VICTORY 72
- JESUS BEARS IT ALL 73
- JUST A DROP OF BLOOD 74
- THE BIBLE 75
- THE DOOR TO A BRIGHTER DAY 76
- THE REASON WHY 77
- THY WILL OH GOD 78

CHRISTMAS TIMES 79
- A LITTLE BOY'S WISH 80
- BORN IN A STABLE 81
- CHRISTMAS ROAD 83
- CHRISTMAS LULLABY 84
- EMMANUEL (GOD WITH US) 85
- I REALLY LOVE CHRISTMAS 87

FACING THE FUTURE

- HAPPY BIRTHDAY JESUS 88
- I'M SO GLAD HIS BIRTHDAY CAME 89
- JESUS BIRTHDAY CAME 90
- LET'S SING OF CHRISTMAS 91
- OUR CHRISTMAS LOVE 92
- OUR SAVIOUR'S BIRTHDAY 93

MORE ABOUT GOD'S POWER 95

- GOD MAKES US ABLE 96
- GOD'S EYES 97
- HEALING 98
- INFINITELY SECURE 99
- IT'S A LONG JOURNEY 100
- JESUS LORD AND SAVIOUR 101
- JEHOVAH 103
- JONAH 104
- MASTER AND SAVIOUR 105
- PLANTING OF THE LORD 106
- POOL OF BETHESDA 107
- SHOUT AND CELEBRATE 108
- THE ANOINTING OIL 109
- THIRTY THREE BIRTHDAYS 110
- THIRTY THREE BIRTHDAYS (PART B) 111
- THE POWER OF GOD 112
- THY WILL OH LORD 113
- TO BE BLESSED 114
- AN EAGLE 115
- DON'T STOP HOPING 116
- GOD 117
- GOD IS THE ONE 118
- GOD IS WITH US 119

OUR PAST 121

- ANNIVERSARY IS GOLDEN 122
- COMING HOME 123
- HOMELAND 125
- IF YOU CROSS THE RIVER 126
- ON A RAILWAY HEADING HOME 127
- LIFE MAY BE ROUGH 129
- SEEDS YOU SOW 131

RELATIONSHIPS 133

- A LIFE'S MISSION 134
- A LITTLE CHILD'S FAITH 135

TABLE OF CONTENTS

    HOLD ON 136
    JUST A PRODIGAL SON 137
    ON THE SEA OF LIFE 138
    OVERCOMERS 139

WRITING FOR A FUTURE 141
    FRESH 142
    HOW FAR IS HEAVEN? 143
    IS EVERYTHING REALLY EVERYTHING? 144
    LIGHT OF LOVE 145
    TIME OR A MIRACLE 146

NIGHT POEMS 147
    A PLACE OF REFUGE 148
    PERFECTED IN HIM 149
    SOOTHING WATERS 150
    THE WIND BLOWS 151
    WAIT FOR HIM 152
    GOD LOVES HIS CHILDREN 153

GOD AND HIS SON 155
    ALL SELF TO THEE OH LORD 156
    LOVING JESUS 157
    JESUS 158
    NEVER ALONE 159
    HE WAS ON TRIAL 160
    THOSE SCARS 161
    GOD'S DIVIDENDS 162
    A FEW DAYS AFTER DEATH 163
    IN THIS WORLD THERE'S JESUS 164
    EVERYONE NEEDS JESUS 165
    I'LL SERVE JESUS 166
    WALKING WITH JESUS 167
    INTO THE FUTURE 168
    FACING THE FUTURE 169

FACING THE FUTURE

MORNING POEMS

FACING THE FUTURE

HOUSE OF POEMS

We live in a dwelling the deed is signed
Some cozy and warm some not very kind.

The body must rest New Hope it will find
Comfort the spirit bring peace to the mind.

A basement to rest on this house we'll see
A firm construction, built splendidly.

Floor, walls, and roof measured to a tee
Could we live in a house, happy and free?

Birth to eternal life strains at the task
Our personal stories beyond any mask.

Each step and choice do we know should we ask?
Retreat to our house we are safe at last.

Tomorrow will tell, the mountains we've climbed
Is our house complete with that peace of mind?

The Master Designer: when He comes will He find?
Our house we live in is a friend all the time.

MORNING POEMS

SOMETIMES IT FEELS STRANGE

Look at troubles in our world everywhere,
Should we be involved? Have we any care?
Crime is like a war—people die full of need,
The answer is the Christ of Calvary.

God's love will help the troubled soul,
We humans need to have things in control.
Look towards the future with hope in sight,
Man is so fragile in daytime or night.

Now is the time to change, before it's too late
Jesus gave help to all, do not hesitate.
Plan to do your own part, don't run and hide
In this world for man, God keeps us satisfied.

FACING THE FUTURE

CIRCLES OF LIFE

When the times of living goes by,
Turn us round, even make us sigh,
Plan each step, if we know how,
Farmers, put your hand on the plough.

Days for man, bringing times of pain,
Some lose their way; some have gain.
We all live under the same sun,
May life treat you kindly—each one.

Comes the night, may you sleep in peace,
Tomorrow comes, time doesn't cease.
We sojourn here, then travel on,
Through this vast home under the sun.

The Master speaks so wise and fine,
Gives hope for all to search and find.
The river of life is flowing free,
God's promise is given to you and me.

How fast we see life go by
First love may even make us cry.
Days pass as we toil and we grow,
In fields of plenty that we've sowed.

MORNING POEMS

WE'VE LIVED, WE'VE LOVED LIFE

We've strolled together on the shore,
Hand in hand more and more,
Laid on the beach at sunset,
Satisfied together since we met.

Watch waves come in from the sea,
Crash on the sand, full and free,
Life we've lived here all our days,
And it's so grand in all its ways.

Another day to live so free,
Time's passing by, we all can see.
Cautiously we step each day in time,
We always walk close to the line.

Each face has its own story,
Complete with the pain and glory.
Each person on earth still has needs,
Some He receives, some He heeds.

Does all mankind shed a tear,
If we don't have comfort here,
We all need love everywhere,
And should want some love to spare.

For a brighter tomorrow we try to prepare,
This vast creation has room to spare.
We're part of the picture; every one must be,
If we wait for tomorrow, then we will all see.

FACING THE FUTURE

MORNING POEMS

THE FURY DOES BLAST

The wind blows the trees to and fro,
The house gave a little creak and sigh.
At the windows in the gale, the leaves did blow,
Holding secure till the storm passed by.

The wind did increase from a gale to a blast,
Swaying trees, will they hold to their roots?
You wonder, through this, will anything last,
Rain comes in fury; we grab our boots.

Hear a big crack of lightning, in the storm,
Thunder rumbles, feel the shake in the floor.
Are the lightning rods secure, are they too worn?
Latch the windows and brace the door.

In the midst of the tumult trees start to fall,
Pieces blowing, shingles off the wall.
On this foundation, the house will stand tall,
Through the night most important we can tell.

The power starts to flicker, then it's gone,
Grab a candle, flashlight, oil lamp strong.
Batteries for the radio, they last how long?
Contact with others, in this storm going on.

Finally time passed by; the storm starts to wane,
Go outside; see the damage done again.
Leaves, branches everywhere down the lane,
The storm passed by, never caused too much pain.

FACING THE FUTURE

NIGHT TIME JOY

Troubles in this world below?
Trust in Jesus, to Heaven we'll go.
No time for fearing or turning back.
Close to Jesus, on the right track.

Joy in nighttime with no delay,
Serving Jesus, night and day.
Sun is shining there in the sky,
Living things grow, little birdies fly.

He poured water and filled the ocean,
Gave to all man His love in motion.
Put the fish of all kinds in the sea,
We follow Him, endlessly.

Sometimes here there's heartache.
When this world might see you break.
Don't let your mind be ensnared.
Remember Jesus—He always cared.

Put trust alone, in your Saviour,
He keeps us in good behaviour.
Everywhere He walks beside you.
Home in Heaven beyond the blue.

MORNING POEMS

OUR ETERNAL HOME

There's a home waiting for all mankind,
Where we'll live forever with Him.
We leave this place, our new home to find,
In His presence alive, and peace within.

We live here below by His mercy.
By grace we are saved, not of works obtained.
Washed in His blood given to men freely.
Joy waits in our new home that we have gained.

The devil has done his best to cheat us.
Just live for now and all of it's gain.
We live for God's treasure, found in Jesus.
Worth more than this world, could ever name.

Dreaming of home, those streets of Glory.
With Jesus our Saviour, Lord, and Friend.
Joint heirs and a mansion, all Heaven's story.
In peace forever, with Jesus no end.

FACING THE FUTURE

MORNING POEMS

POOLS, STREAMS, AND RIVERS

In the valley hot and dry,
In the valley, no time to hide,
Water flows from the sky,
We know God will provide.

Travel on, living for Jesus.
Made of clay by the Master's hands.
Give our lives, He tries to please us.
Jesus came, to save our lands.

To the mountain, on the way
Bad experiences; don't give in.
On mountain peaks hear God say,
In mountain streams we will swim.

Victory in the Holy Spirit.
On mountain tops close to God.
There is a pool, our search will merit.
God walks, on this sod.

You may be striving, with times of teaching.
When we grow in love and grace.
Journey on; God's always reaching.
Dry and thirsty, He waters this place.

To the rivers in the valleys,
Flow the streams from up above.
Into pools, His care shall be.
Never forsaken, He's always love.

FACING THE FUTURE

MORNING POEMS

TOO MANY TROUBLES

When the problems of life lead astray.
All the storms, they want to stay.
No clear answer that you can see.
The time is right for you to plead,
To Jesus—He's there eternally.

Jesus knows everything we go through,
He sees the storms we are facing to.
Every problem in our way,
We face each and every day,
He loves us all, hear him say.

Love overflows through it all.
Even mountains standing tall.
We keep climbing every one,
With help from God's Son,
He is there till the day is done.

It may seem life hurts your dream,
All around there's rocks in the stream,
Everywhere you may turn,
There are always bridges to burn,
Travelling on, we still must learn.

The sunshine is almost gone,
Grab the lifeline and come along.
The night will be so dark,
We'll be safe inside the ark,
With Jesus—nearly time to embark.

FACING THE FUTURE

MORNING POEMS

THE MIND OF GOD

Just to think like You do, Jesus.
All these problems have to go.
By Your power and infinite reason.
To us Your children here below.

We've had the knowledge since creation.
When man fell—this trouble with sin.
From perfection to contemplation.
Living here now, trying to win.

Oh let this mind be in Your children.
They who seek the Father's will.
All our battles, He will win them.
Waiting now, His promise to fill.

It all began as God's creation.
Full of beauty without decay.
Let Your wisdom lead us, Jesus.
To the place of peace—all things OK.

No storm's too great with Jesus.
His peace in the time of storm.
His power and love will please us.
Heaven has conquered all.

FACING THE FUTURE

ANGELS

ANGELS

IN JESUS' HEART

Junkyard angels,
Alone on a quest.
Live another day,
Do their best.
Misfortune, forsaken,
Lost from the view.
They're all human,
And need things too.

How different are they,
Compared to me?
Lost with no hope,
That we can see.
Garbage cans in back alleys,
Alone in the night.
Where no man's a friend,
Nothing seems right.

Do we care, or are we
Governed by greed?
We have a solution,
To fulfil their need.
Goods from our stores,
Love from our shores,
Help with their chores.
Solving their need.

The sun is the same,
The earth for us all.
While there's still time,
Tear down the wall.
Entire lives begin,
And end the same way.
Alone, downhearted,
Nothing more—gone away.

ANGELS

WITH THE ANGELS

In dreams I was flying with the angels,
Where life seemed to be, in their hands,
The wind would blow, yet no bother,
Things were safe, and secure in the hands.

Above the clouds, through gentle breezes,
The air so fresh, so heavenly.
I loved it there, flying with the angels,
None rich or poor, all evenly.

Thoughts of children, so downhearted,
Their lives hurt day by day.
God please help, care for the children,
And all who live in a burdened way.

Time moves on; life called; I answered,
Day by day there's work you must do.
The nighttime dreams, became my vision,
So real, knowing God is always true.

Living today, everywhere there're problems,
Some we change; some things we can't do.
Live the passion; we're all God's children.
Show care for everyone all life through.

FACING THE FUTURE

WHY CAN'T IT ALL BE TRUE?

If the transportation was ready,
Would there be hesitation to go.
Just imagine a trip to Heaven,
Even where astronauts don't know.

A knock on the door some future day,
There stands an angel to whisk you away.
No time to get ready—just get on board,
Appointment with Him they just call Lord.

In the meantime cruising creation,
It seemed that time stood perfectly still.
The Master builder, designer was in sight,
The meeting arranged on a holy hill.

Through clouds, past stars, over rainbows,
This journey more than anything you could plan.
More than a thousand dreams of beauty,
Beyond the realms of time, and man.

"Wait! Do I have a story I can share later?"
I asked one angel, and he did reply,
"It's not yet," but some day soon we will see,
All can travel to that home in the sky.

ANGELS

FACING THE FUTURE

DAY BY DAY

DAY BY DAY

FACING THE FUTURE

A LIFE FULL OF MOUNTAINS

Some people live far from pain,
Seems to be a life full of gain.
Somewhere in tomorrow,
I know they will climb,
One more time,
To God's home divine.

Looking back all around me,
Mountains too high to see,
I've climbed many times,
Lord you helped me try.
Sunshine in an open sky,
Our sweet home by and by.

We journey at a pace,
Part of the human race,
Many climb, trying to keep up.
Land of unclouded day,
Home which angels array,
Where the saints of God stay.

Sometimes all I see,
These mountains surround me,
Thinking when I'm climbing,
Lord is this where I'll die?
God speaks, "Don't cry,
Your new home's in the sky."

ANOTHER TURN IN LIFE'S ROAD

Life can seem short,
To live a hundred or more.
A little while; the time passes,
Ahead, down the road for sure.

Think about loved ones we missed,
Gone now, but memories linger still.
The chore we face with loss,
All we can do is trusting until.

Believing with our whole heart,
The truth of every promise given.
For everyone who believes,
Will stand for sure in Heaven.

We begin life—needing kindness
The days are hard, many fall prey.
Needing helping hands to guide us,
Above darkness and troubles each day.

The warmth from Heaven's portals,
Onward to our eternal home.
We'll soar through time eternal,
To our Father, never alone.

When life's troubles try to seduce you,
Lift your wings of faith and soar.
There's a place of refuge in Jesus,
Between here and Heaven's shore.

A THORN IN THE FLESH

Keep on trying,
Though sometimes in vain.
Keep on believing,
Looking for latter rain.
Keep on looking,
Towards the eastern sky.
Just a short journey,
See Jesus eye to eye.

God made all men,
Formed out of clay.
Gave us life to live,
By faith, His way.
In this flesh you find,
One may stumble around.
Until we touch down,
On Heaven's holy ground.

Life with many trials,
Leaves you looking grim.
Even believing in Jesus,
Its hard to be like Him.
The flesh is a problem,
A thorn in our life.
Jesus will give us victory,
Over our sin and strife.

Doubts and fears beset us,
When from God we turn.
Storms may upset us,
If we can't discern.
We are just human,
With a thorn in the flesh.
Through Jesus we'll conquer,
If we do our best.

DAY BY DAY

BEFORE THE RIVER

Before the river, I stopped to look,
At the journey where many have gone.
There's still time to write in the book,
Many things here, where I belong.

The family and loved ones are still here,
There're loved ones over there, I know.
The choice is mine; I'll stay with no fear,
Enjoy friends, with such love to show.

How that river glistens like glass,
More beauty than we've ever known.
Through this journey all will pass,
The pure in heart, with Jesus, go home.

We depend on our Father above,
Forces try to take from this goal,
He cares for His children by love,
We'll win, and never grow old.

I see that river different than before
Could it be the path to Heaven above?
Time passes by; soon we'll see the door,
Trust in our Saviour who saves by His love.

FACING THE FUTURE

CALLING HIS CHILDREN

To Himself, He calls His children,
Come and drink the waters of life.
O'er mountains, and through the valleys,
He frees from sin and strife.

Holy God You've been forever,
Help us through problems today.
Reach out and walk with Jesus,
Make it home, each step of the way.

Today we're happy in Jesus,
Walk daily with the Master's care.
Sleeping with stars above you,
He'll guide to that land over there.

A kind and loving Father,
Every day His hand supplies.
The Lamb sacrificed at Calvary,
His word will never tell us lies.

The family—God's children—
Are gathering close to home.
Peace and joy through the ages,
Living with Him, never alone.

DAY BY DAY

DELIVERANCE

Deliverance by faith, trusting Him alone,
The power of the cross—sent from God's throne.
Every day we're walking with Him to guide,
Facing life's troubles with strength inside.

Israel was delivered, from Egypt land,
God promised to keep them by His hand.
Mighty armies followed, deep waters to cross,
God in His mercy saved them from loss.

In this life of trials, many trip and fall,
God in His mercy cares for us all.
Overcome temptation, victory all the way,
By His word we're promised a new day.

He's coming for His children, across pages of time
Home from this world, to that land sublime.
Weary pilgrim, hold on, stay steadfast in life,
Climb the last mountain, away from this strife.

God Jehovah delivers, in Him we abide,
God Jehovah delivers, He is our guide.
For deliverance we search in every way,
Trusting in Him gives strength every day.

Over the last mountain, across the way.
No more valleys, no going astray.
Glory rests with those gone before
Look for Jesus—Saviour we adore.

FACING THE FUTURE

DO I STILL NEED MORE?

I have failed a few times, no doubt,
Still I have much cause to shout.
Since Jesus saved my soul,
He cleansed and made me whole.

We are tried and tested sometimes,
Still fishermen, out with the lines.
Working for God because He is,
We can't merit eternal bliss.

Many people have already known,
The sincerity God's love has shown.
Such faith will, always appear,
Presenting Jesus so clear.

Oh yes we still need more,
Wisdom of Jesus whom we adore.
One day in the skies He'll appear,
We'll live with our Saviour so dear.

Our life is complete in Him,
Free from trials of life and sin.
Saved by grace—both young and old,
home with Him, the story is told.

Now through times of testing and trials,
Hold His hand all these miles.
He promised never to leave us alone,
Love will always take us home.

DAY BY DAY

DREAMING OF HEAVEN

Lost in a dream, with visions of love.
Spirit of God came down from above.
Peaceful, merciful, habitation of rest.
By grace, through faith, we'll do our best.

Leave behind everything that brings wrath.
It may lead to sin, fall from our path.
Endure to the end through God's love.
Then home with Jesus in Heaven above.

Time keeps moving ahead day by day.
We step along in a triumphant way.
He made us rich and wise in His plan.
To walk on streets not made by man.

We see trees displayed in their beauty.
Wood used by man, fulfilling their duty.
The earth, made by God, displayed in power.
Cleansed by fire come redemption hour.

Many have found that pathway eternal.
Through the stars, to Heaven supernal.
We who remain, get ready for that time.
When we go to Heaven farther down the line

Some scoff and slander this wonderful home,
May even disbelieve, though living alone.
We should know we're all part of creation.
Accepting our Saviour with no hesitation.

FACING THE FUTURE

ETERNITY

One day, standing, with the choice at hand,
Looking over creation, everything so grand.
God the Creator made this world for man,
While we're living here, lend a helping hand.

On the one hand, we see a broad road so vast,
The end is a pit, where we could be cast.
The other choice, a narrow road so clear,
Sun always shinning from God's home so near.

Into the future we face eternity,
Throngs of people—where will they be?
The saved with Jesus, His children He'll greet,
They take these troubles and lay at His feet.

Whatever we do, wherever we go,
One path to choose, in our life we know.
Others who travel to eternity grand,
Depend on Jesus and His helping hand.

DAY BY DAY

FAMILY BLESSINGS

Jesus came to our house last Sunday afternoon,
Momma sleeping upstairs in the bedroom.
Children playing on the floor, singing up a tune,
Dad heading up to bed, not a bit too soon.

Jesus said," Read your Bible, Have you prayed today?
Take some time to worship. Serve some other way.
You know this world is dying, losing every day,
You could spread My love more, all the way?"

The dinner was delicious, filled right up to the top,
Living with the comfort, love that doesn't stop
Dressed with clean clothes, not new, yet not too bad
We love life, but not the aches and pains we've had.

Then we realize the price to save our souls,
All man in need of help by someone in control.
Must make our decision before we are too old,
Believe in God and His word, the truest story told.

FACING THE FUTURE

FORGIVING

Through the blood of Jesus,
By His mercy and by grace.
Trials can overwhelm you,
Anytime or anyplace.

The Holy Spirit beckons,
Come to Jesus, never alone.
In the presence of the Father,
He'll return and take us home.

Sins forgiven, now we're ready,
Through the blood of Calvary.
A new name and home in glory,
Forevermore, to be set free.

Thou art holy, oh God eternal,
Above the strife this world may bring.
We will be joint heirs with Jesus,
Forevermore with the King.

Day by day, we have encounters,
Seeds of bitterness may grow.
Like Jesus who forgives each trespass,
We forgive and let love show.

DAY BY DAY

GETTING READY TO GO

I'm getting ready to go,
I'm getting ready to go,
With my Lord in control,
He saved and made me whole,
Yes I'm getting ready to go.

He can get you ready to go,
Follow Him—He tells us so.
Saved, sanctified, here below,
Holy Spirit empowers, we know,
Helping us all get ready to go.

Working for the Lord,
With families adored.
God the Father, God the Son,
God the Spirit, three in one,
We're all getting ready to go.

All will be perfect over there,
Here we all have burdens to bear.
Travel all around this world,
He loves every boy and girl,
Everyone is getting ready to go.

FACING THE FUTURE

HAPPY NEW YEAR DECLARATION

Well it finally arrived—a brand new year.
Last year's in history, like turning a page.
We face new territory yet unexplored.
Climb mountains, swim rivers, on our way.

A person who believes, it's a matter of faith.
Another day—an opportunity to seek for truth.
Hoping the sunshine will shine for all,
Hurt and loss will pass, as we search for love.

Some place there's noise; people with high hopes.
Celebration for the joy of a new year,
Territory that's new—never seen it before.
Hold on to truth, you seekers of the light.

May mistakes of our past, bring no hurt at all.
Peace be to the strong—those standing tall.
Help the downhearted, the weak, and the frail.
Life passes along; destinations prevail.

The sun did shine; a full moon lit the night.
Seekers of truth, find the path that's right.
Forward, with a heart full and free.
For mankind to live in this world we see.

We look at every mountaintop we've scaled.
A sailor on the ocean, o'er many seas has sailed.
The white dove of peace, flies high over man,
We can overcome situations—together we can.

DAY BY DAY

HAVE YOU KNOWN FEAR?

So easy to be frightened in a world of turmoil,
Forgetting Jesus once walked on this very soil.
To deliver His children from fear they know,
For Jesus we must live, letting His love show.

Barriers may try to destroy your very soul,
In time Jesus comes and takes full control.
Reviving, inspiring, for us to travel on,
Without fear we sing, a triumphant song.

Finished with this world, will be a glorious day,
Hearing, "Well done," from our Saviour say.
Knowing joy and peace forever then will be,
Through Jesus, now, and through eternity.

No more fear, but His peace I feel,
I now know His wisdom, will show it's real.
One main reason for His love to show,
Count things as lost, to Heaven we will go.

Nothing in this world can replace God's love,
Through Jesus we go, to that happy home above.
Nothing but His Blood ,can wash our sins away,
Such love of our Saviour, will keep us day by day.

FACING THE FUTURE

HE DIED FROM A BROKEN HEART

Down on skid row,
> the streets aren't very kind,

People who've lost hope,
> many walking blind.

If they could see the light,
> from the windows up above,

Know that someone, somewhere,
> could show a little love.

Sell love on the corners,
> where lights are low,

Days with sunshine don't matter,
> this way they go.

There is someone who loves them—
> really loves them true,

The Baby who came at Christmas,
> can be their Christ too.

In church for service,
> sleep and worry cloud the mind,

Needing His forgiveness,
> a cleansing stream this time.

Put our hope in our Saviour
> where else can we go?

He died on the cross—
> the Bible tells us so.

They cried have no mercy,
> as the crowds pressed Him so,

Then He stretched out His hands,
> to the cross He did go.

The same little Baby
> we remember at Christmas time,

There on mount Calvary,
> laid His heart on the line.

I WANT TO SERVE MY LORD

I want to, not have to, serve Jesus as Lord,
I thank Him for lifting, my sinful load.
Now I know that Jesus, can satisfy,
He has gone to prepare a home on high.

I want to, not have to, serve Jesus as Lord,
One day I was lost, my life overboard.
Then Jesus, my Saviour, reached down by His love,
Started my journey to that home above.

I want to, not have to, serve Jesus as Lord,
Now I am travelling with Him, on life's road.
Knowing that Jesus will see me through,
If I bear my cross for Him do what I must do.

If you want to not have to serve Jesus as Lord,
Know Jesus will help you, along life's rocky road.
To all who believe Him, redemption's applied,
Their lives will always be, with Jesus to abide.

These hands of mine praise His holy name,
We turn to find answers in life's game?
Jesus' hands were nailed, to an old rugged cross,
Now we can be saved from a life full of loss.

On the rugged cross, Jesus paid the cost,
Once and for always, Jesus died for the lost.
Delivering from sin, setting us free,
Giving us salvation, look to Him and see.

FACING THE FUTURE

IF YOU CROSS THE RIVER

If you cross the river, before I go,
Look for my dad; tell him we miss him so.
Walk with him in glory, on streets so fair,
Tell Him soon we're coming, God's love to share.

Watch the stars as they twinkle, in God's big sky,
They'll send a message, through the sweet by and by.
For us who still labour, in this world below,
Waiting for our turn, when it's our time to go.

We look at flowers, the trees on the ground,
Everything in its season—this is what we've found.
Beauty of the sky, clouds that water the soil,
Gives life for the harvest, it's true as they toil.

Maybe you've lost a loved one, a mother or a dad,
Leaving comes too early, making us feel sad.
Over there with Jesus, in that land so fair,
A land called Heaven, His love they will share.

By the river side, in the still of the day,
I stood to see the light shine—a magnificent array.
It was so beautiful—a double rainbow,
Stretching from shore to shore, so fine, so low.

While I stood in silence, to view the site so fine,
Many memories and words raced through my mind,
Even though we've parted, on this earth below,
One day we'll live in that land, to part no more.

DAY BY DAY

JUST UP ON THE HILL ON THE OTHER SIDE

Through the valley we walk,
    sometimes without choice,
Our souls oh so burdened
    and heavy with care.
When we lift our eyes,
    towards the eastern sky,
We see the King coming
    to take His bride away.

Just up on the hill,
    on the other side,
We'll get a closer glimpse
    of our eternal home.
Sun's always shining;
    dark clouds blow by,
Closer to Jesus
    coming for us through the sky.

Here the road may be rocky,
    and feet get worn,
We must keep on pressing
    to our eternal home.
Through all things with Jesus,
    He gives a crown,
To those who keep on striving
    till they reach the holy ground.

Sometimes the battle rages,
    and the way grows dark,
Yet the soldiers for Jesus
    are safe in the ark.
The enemy has been conquered;
    a new day has begun,
Now we'll just live with Jesus,
    God's chosen Son.

FACING THE FUTURE

LIFE IS A MIRACLE

At the start of a miracle, may be a lot of pain,
Sometimes like the flowers, waiting for the rain.
On your way through life, journeying here,
Believing He gives help, in each trial and fear.

I've been here many times, so far in my life,
Thanked Him for deliverance from the strife.
Each new day I'd never make it without Him,
Through life's struggles, we all want to win.

Ahead you might see a mountain standing there,
Or maybe darkness comes out from everywhere.
With faith inside, we can see the fountain wide,
If we drink from that water, we can be satisfied.

God's Spirit can dwell within all who believe,
He'll help us through, and never deceive.
Give strength inside, for life's journeys here,
Assurance we can be part of His family so dear.

Then looking back someday on our journey here,
We'll see Him through every trial and fear.
Knowing it's worth it, just to have His love,
Live with Him forever, in that home up above.

DAY BY DAY

LIFE TO LIVE OVER AGAIN

The joy and satisfaction this world can give,
Exists for the moment, caring little how you live.
Only two masters, we choose between,
Our decision plans our path, as we have seen.

See all the people—for this world they live,
Knowing little about Jesus—the love He has to give.
I am thankful I found Him and His eternal home,
We will live forever, rejoicing round God's throne.

If I had my life to live over again,
Would I still walk, the pathway of sin?
Feel convicted, or have a sense of shame,
With Jesus to cleanse, over and over again?

Would I still welcome Spring as growing time?
With the grass getting green, the flowers so fine.
The snow melting fast, filling waterways,
Life everywhere hatching with the days.

The joy in the Summer, the sunshine so warm,
The birds and the bees, singing in a swarm.
This makes us happy, each year we see it again,
Live with the seasons, feel the growing pain.

Life to live over, in the Fall things may end,
Vibrant colours of harvest, beauty they send.
Cool days of Winter, wisdom's purpose refined,
Orderly we move along, beauty waits so fine.

FACING THE FUTURE

LOVE

Just sitting around the open fire,
Reminiscing over the past year.
Realizing the time so quickly went by,
Some in sadness, some in cheer.

I know the rain keeps things growing,
Every time the raindrops fall.
The roots of life are always showing,
They will fade again—time will tell.

The flowers which bloom in the Summer sun,
Have faded now for awhile.
While we enjoy the Winter fun,
They'll return again Spring style.

The cold way some may treat our heart,
Leaves us feeling empty inside.
Now I've found your love plays a part,
I realize some feelings are meant to hide.

Tomorrow once more we'll be,
Sharing love again for a time.
Even though outside the cold North wind blows,
It won't keep our love off line.

Just like the snowflakes falling around,
Out there lying still on the ground.
We shared love last year and this year still,
Christmas celebration, all around.

I knew our love like a flower would grow,
Sometimes it might fade for a while.
Even though it moves when the Winter wind blows,
In Spring it comes again in style.

DAY BY DAY

LOVE IS THE ONLY ANSWER

Your skin may be red,
>white, or black,

If you're serving Jesus,
>your on the right track.

So many roads—
>be sure you're on the right one,

Then we'll travel towards
>our heavenly home.

You know this God
>we serve from on high,

He's got the power;
>even makes the sun shine.

He made the moon
>and the stars above,

He made them all,
>for man, by His love.

In this life
>you may travel many places,

By your own strength—
>that's sure no disgrace.

With God's help
>we can go really far,

He's coming
>faster than a shooting star.

Got to climb that mountain,
>till we reach the top,

Keep on climbing;
>give it all you got.

Trusting in Jesus,
>He'll help all the way,

Making a home
>up there beyond the blue.

FACING THE FUTURE

IN THE SKY AND ALL YEAR AROUND

THE MELODY OF LIFE IS THE SOUND

DAY BY DAY

MELODY OF LIFE

He picks up the pieces,
Of a life torn apart.
He picks up the pieces,
When you have a burdened heart.
He'll pick up the pieces,
Of one who looks to Him.
He'll heal and mend them again.

He picks up the pieces,
When your dreams are all gone.
Searching for what pleases,
Pressure moves them along.
He'll put them back together,
Fast and firm on the rock.
Keeping them secure for all time.

While the storms pass us by,
So fierce and strong.
Making us wonder why,
Life can seem so wrong
Don't give up or turn away,
He'll pick up the pieces again,
His love will show us how to stay strong.

We can get a fresh new start,
Give all our troubles over to Him.
Tomorrows with a change of heart,
We know we're bound to win,
New sunrise brings us warmth,
Our new pathway with light,
Now we know for sure, He is the way.

FACING THE FUTURE

MAN AND CREATION

The time of man passed by,
Millions of years it seems,
So strange knowing how far,
We've advanced in life's streams.
Then compared to the past
Where were the signs
Of any parallel then and now,
To the last hundred years of time?

Especially in the age of revolution,
In the transportation and production line.
Now we see the advancement daily,
In this technology frame of mind.
It jumps ahead by leaps and bounds,
By the minute we hear notice,
Another whistle; another missile,
Wondering is this intelligence's voice?

Even in more primitive areas,
Like hunting, gathering, fishing,
Other necessary items for survival.
Would it take us a million years of wishing?
To learn how to even make a gun.
Or other useful weapons or a school.
For sure, running around with a club,
Doesn't seem an effective hunting tool.

Still we're here in this age,
Learning so much about the past,
The history and family tree,
So unique, the way things can last.
We'll grow and invest for tomorrow,
Even though it may bring sorrow,
If only we could put our faith in love,
A way for no one having to borrow.

DAY BY DAY

PANIC OR PEACE

When the strain of life, and tension, nears,
Do we cringe and hide—give in to our fears?
There is no doubt we all need our space,
Yet in everyday life, things get in our face.

Calm and assurance, within me remains,
There's a place of rest, secure, with no pains.
Storms and confusion, crash close all around,
Still anchored in Jesus to solid ground.

Within I seek, for that hope to belong,
Force that prevails sees where I stand strong,
All people are here, all creation so grand,
On this plain of life, we all must stand.

For peace! For peace! the cry of my heart,
Live and respect life—a treasure in part.
The hope of survival, above the mountain peak,
We climb through life, for truth we seek.

A seed grows today, seems so fine,
Tomorrow's tests, thorns and thistles entwine.
Survive; seek life; tomorrow will come,
Be kind to yourself—live for God's Son.

FACING THE FUTURE

POOR AND NEEDY

The poor and needy search for water,
There is none, there is none.

Their tongues are parched with thirst,
There is none, there is none.

The Lord God will answer them,
The Lord God will not forsake them.

He will do it so they will be free,
They will know that He is their God.

He will make rivers flow on barren heights,
And springs flow in the valleys.

He will turn the desert into pools of water,
The parched ground into springs.

So that God's people will see and know,
They may consider and understand.

The hand of the Lord can do this,
The Holy One of Israel will create it.

Keep on believing—God can do anything,
He will help in the time of need.

When times are not always friendly,
He'll be there; His word tells us so.

DAY BY DAY

RISE AND SHINE

In the morning when I rise,
And look at the day
Before me, I wonder,
What is planned for today?

You read the newspapers,
All the disheartening events.
Taking place all around,
Causing the earth to lament.

To believe in this world,
Remains such a strong need.
For the Bible, God's Holy Words,
Tells all man to heed.

What was going to happen, happened.
All events that were told,
By the holy men of God,
Are coming true as gold.

Prophecies were delivered,
Through these holy men of old.
Told us about the future,
To get ready and stand bold.

In the beginning of times
A prophecy about a Child,
Born in the manager,
On Christmas day, meek and mild.

God sent a Saviour to the people,
This prophecy was fulfilled.
When Jesus was born,
Even though He would be killed.

God sent His First Born Son,
Born of a woman.
This Mighty Man was coming.
The Word says He's the one,

SEARCHING, SEARCHING

I searched all around, all over town,
Sometimes even friends couldn't be found.
Then Jesus I met—no more losing ground,
We're together forever, the King and I

Sometimes hard times, like songs with no rhymes,
Out of place, not fitting in with the times.
Then Jesus I found—filled in all the lines,
Now I'm standing firm on my own two feet.

Through the dark night, in search of some light,
Out of the darkness and seeking what's right.
Searching for that place with all my might,
Listening carefully for the Master's call.

It's Jesus I've found! Yes, Jesus I've found,
This friendship so sweet all around.
Once out of place, on sinking ground,
Now safe with this man from Galilee.

You may look without end, needing a friend,
I believe this man, your hurt He'll mend.
Step out of the shadows; new hope He'll send,
Walk to the light, there's peace evermore.

Connect to the Vine, that new life divine,
Living in the Spirit, its free and sublime,
A branch of the Vine, healthy all the time,
Bearing fruit for the Master, and living free.

DAY BY DAY

THE CRIMSON VALLEY

Have you walked, the crimson valley
Where God's mercy, flows so free?
There He washes, all sin away,
Frees from sin, eternally.

There is sunshine, o'er the mountain,
So full and bright, that all can see.
If we will only, walk with Jesus,
He gives life—pure and free.

On this pathway, all can travel,
Even though, it's sometimes hard.
Because His blood was shed for all men,
His promises, are never marred.

You can find peace, with contentment,
And a journey, that satisfies.
His hand is always, there to guide you,
Toward happy, Heavenly skies.

So go on your way, rejoicing,
Keep trusting, and you will find.
The time you spent, in the valley,
Was planned by God, in His time.

FACING THE FUTURE

THE SUNSHINE IS YOURS AND MINE

So let the sun shine, shine, shine,
The stars in the night, twinkle so fine.
Let the sun shine, shine, shine,
On this earth, of yours and mine.

Wake up in the morning; get out of bed,
Working hard every day, just to be fed.
We know when it's Friday, we receive pay,
Giving it all we got, working God's way.

Work for the dollar, brings pain some way,
Sun up to sun down, every working day.
Try to survive here, in the sunshine,
No surprise, we're all born, to stay on line.

With the truth to help, brighten the way,
We keep going on, though some things dismay.
Always the dark, before the morning light,
The worst thing is to fall, and lose our sight.

All the world's children, have a right to shine,
With love and hope, always there, all the time.
Climb the mountains, cross the deepest seas,
Till we make it home, in the summer breeze.

DAY BY DAY

THERE IS STILL HOPE

If you've been turning the tread mill of sin,
Realizing the state that you have been in.
The life you are living needs one true way,
To have satisfaction, a love to never sway.

People are losing hope and trust every day,
They are losing what the Scriptures say.
Jesus Christ is Lord, to all who believe,
If in trouble, to God we must cleave.

The time is coming, when everyone shall see,
There was enough time to prepare for eternity.
There is light shining, in the darkness and toil,
To help us do it for Jesus—it will never spoil.

FACING THE FUTURE

THEY CAME TO CHURCH WITH DADDY ONE MORE TIME

They came to church with Daddy one more time,
Though it's been a while, they all looked fine.
The prayers of the loved ones, on the line,
Hear them call on Jesus name, one more time.

They start a little family, the baby's cry,
Mom and Dad so happy, thanking Jesus on high.
They have another baby boy, by and by,
Two children run and play, with dreams to fly.

Jesus loves the little children; He's their King,
Through church windows, hear them sing.
All gathered together, God's sweet praises ring,
Worshipping God's Son, our soon coming King.

Time goes by, and time for Jesus seems to wane,
So much to do, love for God starts to drain.
The worlds distractions; love divided—not the same,
Staying true to God and praising His Holy Name.

Some day when all the family's come together,
At the marriage supper of the Lamb, with our Father.
Free from all cares of life, and stormy weather,
In church with our Daddy, once more together.

DAY BY DAY

THROUGH TROUBLED WATERS

Today, your path may be,
        through rough waters,
Keep your eyes
        always on the Lord.
Then tomorrow
        when all trials have been finished,
We'll know it was Him,
        by us all the time.

He'll bring you through,
        life's tests and trials,
No matter what
        you may be going through.
He speaks peace,
        in the stormy weather,
And brings us through
        troubled waters again.

Day by day, you know
        every good work is tested,
It takes all your strength
        to stand for Him.
When you look at life,
        and it's few short minutes,
It makes eternity, living with God,
        so much to win.

Someday,
        the rapture or the grave awaits us,
I pray the glory, of going home,
        so much to win.
The rush of angel's wings
        coming for His children,
Will cause praise, on lips
        of those who look for Him.

FACING THE FUTURE

TRY AND TRY

Who daily try and try, never to forget.
Trying to be humble, still seeming in vain,
To survive the challenge, seems like a game,
To those who haven't crossed that finish line yet,

The sun doesn't change—at least it's there,
You see it in the mornings, if the day is clear.
Exploding burst of light, heat in its power,
Reach out; touch it; feel the warmth each hour.

Still a happy day, even in the rain,
The flowers and the buds, start to bloom again.
All these things so real; How much do we pay?
Our systems so fine, need the sun's ray.

Sure life needs money, and other things too,
Help the wheels turn, all things come true.
Nice to have peace, and skies always blue,
We must keep trying, until our day is through.

DAY BY DAY

WHERE IS HEAVEN?

Heaven's across the bridge of doubting,
Over troubled waters of fear.
To the other side, through salvation,
With all God's promises so clear.

Sometimes I've wandered without a plan,
Not sure where I was going.
There was this faith in God above,
Heard Jesus' call, tHis love was showing.

Can you tell me the answer to this question,
"Where is this place called Heaven above?"
Jesus said He's going to prepare it,
He'll take His church there by His love.

Even though the skies maybe dark and cloudy,
Waters are storm-tossed to and fro.
Can't stay focused on times around us,
Eyes on Jesus, He'll show us how to go.

He'll return for His bride adorned and ready,
Take her to the marriage supper of the Lamb.
Must get ready for that day with Him,
Then we'll reunite, with God in glory land.

FACING THE FUTURE

WORKING FOR JESUS

There is still time to be working,
Jesus hasn't returned yet.
There's always the evil one lurking,
God knows, and will never forget.

There's always work—no hesitation,
Do our best, save souls from Hell.
Living our life with God's salvation,
Living water, from deep in the well.

Life is always an adventure,
To all, who know the Lord.
The task sometimes, is not sure,
He'll help, since His love we've adored.

The darkness will soon be setting,
Time is going by each day.
Thanking God for not forgetting,
Our lives are changed God's way.

JESUS SECTION

JESUS SECTION

FACING THE FUTURE

JESUS CARES

What do you think I should do?
Living a life trying to stay true.
The Lord knows how I've tried,
Always, to this flesh I have died.

Where can I go to find someone?
To help like God's chosen Son.
Answers are in the palm of His hands,
For the burdened, all across these lands.

Oh Lord, just to see your face,
I'm just a sinner, saved by grace.
Nothing that I could ever obtain,
Would ever compare to Jesus' name.

Just to know, that you are God,
Helps us, Lord, walk on this sod.
Even though we have a plan,
You know we're just mere men.

I cannot count all the ways,
God's love always stays.
Many things we leave behind,
To the future, where all is kind.

Times we wonder, what will last,
Memories linger, from the past,
Then we pray, "Dear Lord, please come.
We've placed our faith, in your dear Son."

JESUS SECTION

JESUS CLIMBED THAT MOUNTAIN

With Jesus I'm climbing that mountain,
There's nothing I can't do with Him.
Through the mountains, oh so tall,
Wait on the Lord, climbing steadily.

With Jesus I'm drinking at the fountain,
There is no end to that heavenly flow.
When I'm thirsty, He always satisfies,
All our lifetime, He's always in control.

With Jesus as Saviour, I now live for Him,
Here in this life and forever we win.
Through all the trials, He's gone before,
Trusting in His grace, until Heaven's shore.

Jesus is the person everyone longs to see,
When you've decided to live eternally.
One day He'll return to gather His bride,
Everyone who's living on the Lord's side.

Lift your hands, praise His holy name.
For God is good and always is the same.
He loved us then, made a home on high.
Through life, to the sweet by and by.

FACING THE FUTURE

JESUS DIED FOR ALL

On a lonely hill,
Nailed to a cross.
Our Saviour was dying,
Paying the cost.
For you and for me,
Jesus answered the call.
He shed His own blood,
His precious blood, for all.

I don't imagine,
Many loved Him dear.
Who had gathered,
Round about Him there.
Who might have been thinking,
If this is really Him?
What a heavy burden,
He bore, for our sin.

God planned Him as Saviour,
Years before He had died,
Too save us from sin,
He had nothing to hide.
No shame or guilt in Him,
He died there just the same.
A way—we can enter in,
Too glorify God's name.

JESUS SECTION

JESUS IS ON MY SIDE

I'm just so glad, Lord,
        to know, You're on my side,
I'm just so glad, Lord,
        to know, You're by my side.
When I wake in the morning,
        You're standing near,
Hear Your children praying,
        see a falling tear.

I'm just so glad, Lord,
        to know, you're on my side,
In mornings early light,
        you'll safely guide.
In the nighttime,
        when I feel so all alone,
You reassure me,
        that I'm one of your own.

I'm just so glad, Lord,
        to know, you're on my side,
When discouragement comes,
        and I begin to slide.
You pick me up, encourage,
        and start me off anew,
Your word shows me,
        all the way through.

I'm just so glad to know, Lord,
        you're on my side,
At work, rest, or play,
        you'll always guide.
When life here is ended,
        and it's time to go home,
You made a place, where
        we'll never be alone.

FACING THE FUTURE

JESUS OUR EXAMPLE

Yes we know
      what Jesus went through,
When His world
      seemed to break in two.
Never once
      did He fail or turn back,
The way He wants us to stay,
      right on track.

Do we follow the example,
      Jesus gave on earth?
Does His light shine in our lives,
      from our birth?
Do we walk in His light,
      daytime and night?
An example of His love—
      doing what is right?

His journey on earth,
      began in Bethlehem
To Calvary,
      where they nailed Him to the cross.
He lived His life, a pattern
      for mankind to see,
We can follow in His ways,
      living full and free.

He gave His life to save us,
      from dying in our sins,
True if we choose,
      to always follow Him.
Never give up,
      even though burdened with care,
Live through it all;
      He'll every burden share.

JESUS SECTION

JESUS' PRESENCE

In the presence of Jesus,
Just want to fellowship,
Holy Spirit moving,
Draw me into worship.

Make me a vessel,
Living for You,
With Your love and teaching,
All things true.

Holy vessels for You,
Your beauty we see,
Filled with Your love,
Deeper than the sea.

Filled with Your power,
As full as can be,
Living for now,
And for all eternity.

FACING THE FUTURE

THE VINE

Connected to the lifeline,
As branches, we are,
The life in the Spirit,
Both near and far,
The branch is healthy,
Bearing fruit for Thee,
Attached to the vine,
In this world staying free.

Soon with Him we shall be,
His bride clothed with purity,
Beauty of His love,
Full and free.
Live forever in glory.
In weakness,
your mercy we need;
Fellowship indeed.

JESUS SECTION

JESUS WALKED ON THE WATER

Jesus walked on the water, Jesus walked on the land,
Jesus walked on the water; Jesus walked on the land.
Jesus walked on the water; Jesus walked on the land.
Dear Lord, I pray, lend me Your hand.

They were out on a little boat sailing, over to the other side.
Then the stormy waves battered; Jesus walked to the boat side.
The disciples were fearful thinking a spirit they did see.
Peter cried, "Lord if it's You, help me walk on this sea."

Can you see dark clouds of troubles; life's storms pressing so.
Those waves are high and boisterous, on those waves you gotta go.
Try and see beyond your troubles, to the Master's open arms.
He will help you to survive here, coping with all your alarms.

Someday soon He's coming across the pages of time,
We'll see the sun shining; we'll be standing in line.
He said, "Be ye watching; keep your eyes above."
He gives grace and mercy and saves us by His love.

FACING THE FUTURE

YES VICTORY

It is in the valleys,
Where the real race is run,
The eternal values,
Of our new life are begun.
Jesus brings the victory,
Over Satan's snares,
Making known to all,
The love He shares.

Though many times it seems,
I had fallen so low,
There is always Jesus,
To whom we may go.
When Satan like a storm,
Strives to overcome,
Turn to Jesus in trouble,
He's God's chosen Son.

I've got the road map,
To my home on high,
Where Jesus is preparing,
To come through the sky.
Live forever with Him,
On the hallelujah side,
No more sin—just living,
With nothing more to hide.

Yes it is victory I needed,
Sweet victory I got,
To live with Jesus,
On a heavenly plot.
In this world we find out,
God will always provide,
Giving us the victory,
In that we can confide.

DEATH AND RESURRECTION

DEATH AND RESURRECTION

FACING THE FUTURE

BETRAYED TO CLAIM VICTORY

It was told many times to His disciples,
It was mentioned to others as well.
Those who betrayed Him took notice,
He would have victory over death and Hell.

He lived life, a Saviour to many,
One followed Him, lies He would tell.
Who betrayed Him, fulfilling God's promise,
Jesus saves our souls from Hell.

Jesus Christ will live on forever,
Gave life on the cross for our souls.
Love that would never forsake us,
Eternal promise, a life full of goals.

Three days in the grave planned for Jesus,
Dead and buried, for all men to see.
Plans for death and resurrection,
Men can be saved for eternity.

According to the Word, time's approaching.
When we will see, the coming King of Kings.
Return in a cloud as He promised,
For this same Jesus, the angels sing.

Signs have shown—soon on the horizon,
Everything in place, since Jesus came.
Now by grace all men have salvation,
Believe in Jesus and confess His Holy Name.

DEATH AND RESURRECTION

JESUS BEARS IT ALL

Cast all your burdens on Jesus,
This is what He wants you to do.
All the worries in this life,
Jesus gladly bears them too,
All the sin and all the strife.

Sometimes fears may set in,
Trying to test your soul.
That's the time—yield to Jesus,
To the one who makes us whole,
Cast all your cares on Him.

Heavy laden—our Saviour at Calvary,
The reason He came from above
Bearing man's sin and turmoil,
God planned it by His love,
We can win in Jesus name.

In this world we have one main chore,
Seek the perfect will of God.
He died for all at Calvary.
Leading the way the saints have trod,
Casting all our cares on Him.

FACING THE FUTURE

JUST A DROP OF BLOOD

Just a drop of thy blood,
To wash my sins away.
Just a glimpse of God,
He will save you today,

The life I once lived,
When I walked in sin.
Jesus shed His blood to give,
A cleansing stream within.

The pictures of my past sins,
He now has washed away.
Jesus love will forever last,
A foundation never to sway.

All the cares of tomorrow,
Are never mine anymore.
Jesus bears all sorrow,
Delivers forevermore.

Just a drop of Thy blood,
Along life's troubled road.
Your words my life has heeded,
Heading to my heavenly abode.

The task is to avoid disaster,
For all man, there is a way.
Must give our all to the Master,
He'll save, and show us the way.

DEATH AND RESURRECTION

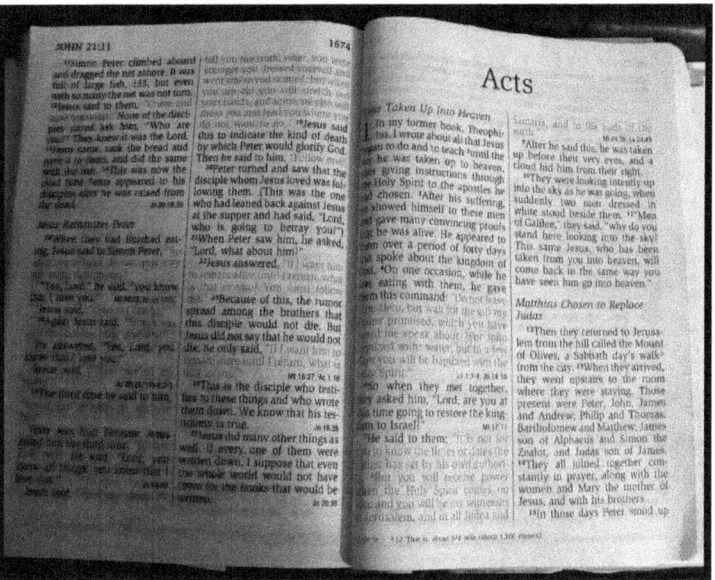

THE BIBLE

Oh how inspired the Word of God is to me,
Knowing, directly from God it has come.
No other book plans for our eternity,
Jesus shining brighter than the sun.

Just reading the Scriptures so true,
Satisfies all the longings of our soul.
For our survival, it tells us what to do,
Letting Jesus, our Saviour, have full control.

In the pages of glory, all power does tell,
Of the God, whom all men should know.
If thirsty, we drink from the living well,
Cleanse all sin and shame, by its flow.

I know its fullness, all men can see,
The blood from the cross—Jesus shed.
Atonement for our souls—so free.
Safe forever in His arms, being led.

FACING THE FUTURE

THE DOOR TO A BRIGHTER DAY

Have the blood of Jesus applied,
On the doorpost of your heart.
Showing to all the world,
Jesus lives in here.

We must bear our cross daily,
For Jesus, and do our part.
Knowing all mankind,
Would find the victory.

We may bear reproach,
Gladly for our Saviour in love.
Living for Him as we journey on,
Nothing for vainglory anymore.

In this world there's nothing to gain,
We give all our life to Jesus name.
In affliction, God is still the same,
Our eternal home is waiting above.

We serve Jesus Christ as our Lord,
He's passed all these tests.
So that we as mere men,
May see the way home.

We know the way, made by God,
Through Jesus we have eternal life.
He is the door, leading us home,
We shall walk in that brighter day.

DEATH AND RESURRECTION

THE REASON WHY

At the foot of the cross,
        I stood one day,
Having nothing that words,
        could possibly say.
Except to thank Jesus
        for dying that way,
Receiving life,
        more abundantly.

Legs that held,
        began to quiver and shake,
I felt self and pride,
        began to break.
On my knees,
        feelings couldn't fake,
To accept Jesus,
        my life had to break.

My life then renewed,
        from sin I abhor,
My destination's changed,
        to heaven's shore.
The living Saviour,
        as pilot forevermore,
The joy He is offering!
        This friend, I adore.

If you have never known,
        the Lord died for you,
Never accepted,
        God's power so true,
Jesus came to the earth,
        our sin to subdue,
The cross at Calvary,
        gives life anew.

FACING THE FUTURE

THY WILL OH GOD

I have no other
    life to live,
Passing through
    this world below.
Jesus came,
    a ransom to give,
That we all
    to Heaven can go.

We're born
    with this understanding,
New life came
    from Heaven above.
Then sin came,
    death it was handing,
God's will was to save us,
    by His love.

It is always there,
    just for the asking,
To know God's will—
    His plan divine.
Evil hides its path,
    using masking
To blind from seeing God,
    all the time.

Trusting forever
    in Jesus,
He's sufficient
    for our every need.
We should seek Him;
    He died to save us,
Put within us,
    His faith like a seed.

CHRISTMAS TIMES

CHRISTMAS TIMES

CHRISTMAS TIMES

FACING THE FUTURE
A LITTLE BOY'S WISH

Just the other night I followed the main line downtown, to do my Christmas shopping, most everyone was found, rushing and tearing in such a hurried way. I know that many people were there on that holiday.

Just as I walked through the doors of the biggest store that I found, I spotted just a little lad sitting down there on the cold cold ground. I asked Him what He was doing? Then He replied, "Kind sir, I'm just here waiting for Christmas eve. You see my dad doesn't have a job, you know, and money just seems so scarce, why everything we had in the house is now gone for drink; it's a curse! Mother works so hard, you see I've got three brothers younger than I, so I'm just down here begging for money as men pass by."

I know everybody wants to buy a special gift, to give to their darling at this time of year but there is some one somewhere needing more than money can buy, the love that they're needing is written in the sky.

I offered to buy Him a hot drink and something to eat, but He refused and said, "Do you think maybe I could have the money instead, you know I've got three brothers younger than I and I'd like to take home to my little brothers a present they could use, and let them know that this Christmas time is really a time for love". Well I passed Him a dollar and it seemed like such a shame, for as I walked away I fell the cold and the fallen rain, that little boy outside that Christmas store lit so bright was cold lonely and shivering on that lovely Christmas night.

Everywhere I was shopping, people were having such a time, with so many decisions, wondering what they were going to buy.

But that little lad was waiting just run down so low,

He didn't have any plans, anywhere to go.

As I walked back out through the doors almost at closing time, I looked and couldn't see Him, for I still had Him on my mind, I wanted to take Him home for a bed and something to eat. I'm sure my wife wouldn't mind, for that's who Jesus came to seek. Instead I found a little note with a few words scribbled on it, in just a little boy's language, it was kind of like a song. so as I picked up the little paper and read these words, I knew the angels must have been here or else it was just a dream. "Won't you tell my daddy that Jesus came for Him, Christmas time is for loving not for the drink of men you know our love will always be the right kind, if we celebrate with Jesus His birthday at Christmas time".

CHRISTMAS TIMES

BORN IN A STABLE

Born in a stable in Bethlehem
To save sinful man.
Gave His life, to atone,
So we'd never walk alone

He made Heaven and Earth,
Creation of beauty, from its birth.
Coming again, King Of Kings,
All creation's, choir sings.

Hallelujah! Praise to Your name,
Hallelujah! You are everything.
All my life is in Your hands,
Living God, we're in Your plans.

Down an old, country road,
Driving a snow-covered, winter load,
I heard the Christmas bells ringing
Loud and clear, choirs singing.

You, oh God, make this joy clearer,
Celebrating Your birth, we hold You dearer.
Jesus, we're glad to know You,
Especially, that Your love is true.

Bringing Christmas joy, to every girl and boy,
Cheer and good will, peace You deploy.
With You Jesus, we can loudly sing,
Peace on Earth, to all you bring.

FACING THE FUTURE

CHRISTMAS TIMES

CHRISTMAS ROAD

Where is this baby child?
We're looking everywhere.
Where is the Holy Child,
God sent to burden bear?

We've been riding for days,
Seeking hard all the time.
Seen His star, heard His ways,
Following the King, to make Him mine.

This is the road we must travel,
Sometimes we're walking on and on.
Lots of mountains, plains unravel,
Seek Him, all the way home.

We'll stand with Him, until forever,
He is the one the future needs.
We'll stand with Him through stormy weather,
Then live in peace—His words we heed.

All our passion, love, and living,
To this child, God's Son, we'll give.
Seek and find Him; life He's giving,
Save us all, new life we'll live.

FACING THE FUTURE

CHRISTMAS LULLABY

On a long starry night,
    over the hills of old Judea
Came the cries
    of little lambs being born.
Some were for sacrifice,
    only those without blemish,
Atonement for man's sins—
    they paid the cost.

Sleep baby Jesus,
    in the arms of Your mamma,
You'll need your rest,
    for strong You will be.
Soon You'll grow to a boy,
    hear the call of your Father,
Be the lamb sacrifice,
    to set men free.

The Lamb on the cross,
    was the baby in the manger,
Born in the stable,
    on that first Christmas morn.
Angels, shepherds, wise men—
    shield the babe from all danger.
While Mary rocked
    the baby who was born.

Soon some starry night,
    when men rest from their labour,
O'er the hills of time,
    we'll hear our Master call.
If we believe the sacrifice,
    try and help our neighbour,
We'll rise triumphant,
    to our mansion after all.

CHRISTMAS TIMES

EMMANUEL (GOD WITH US)

Emmanuel, the baby, there in a stable born,
The baby Jesus, on that happy Christmas morn.
Mary, told by angels of the King that she bore,
The Son of God, our Saviour, lives forevermore

The baby born that day, walks His Father's way,
On earth a carpenter, for souls of men He prays.
Grows in wisdom of His Father, He must obey,
To the cross, on the hill, born to die this way.

A teacher, a preacher, an evangelist so true,
The Lamb of God, who brought, salvation to you.
Born in a stable, from birth, a friend to man,
Lived His life an example, to show the Master's plan.

The baby is the Lamb, of our God who came,
The bridegroom for the bride, our coming King.
At the trumpet call, we'll rise and live with Him,
Ready to meet the Son of God, who lives again.

While ages roll in Heaven, by His side forevermore,
Serve Him, soon we cross to Heaven's golden shore.
We'll join the angels, all the prophets of old,
With joy wise men still seek Him, now and evermore.

FACING THE FUTURE

CHRISTMAS TIMES

I REALLY LOVE CHRISTMAS

I really love Christmas,
      really! Love Christmas.
It brings
      so much fun and joy.
I really love Christmas,
      really! Love Christmas.
With lights, celebrations,
      and Jesus boy.

When I was a little child,
      presents were fun.
We'd look towards Christmas
      with hope and cheer.
As the years went by,
      we celebrated God's Son.
Seeing the changes
      in Christmas each year.

There's this wonderful peace
      it brings inside.
Makes me sing,
      "Peace on earth good will to men."
This baby, born with love,
      we'll never hide.
How He loves us all—
      came to free from sin.

We see the star in the sky,
      "Oh holy night," we cry.
Its Christmas time, in our heart,
      His love so true.
Baby in a manager,
      this was God's reason why.
Wise men seek Him,
      to that home beyond the blue.

FACING THE FUTURE

HAPPY BIRTHDAY JESUS

Happy birthday,
        Jesus,
Happy birthday,
        Lord.
We're just so
        thankful,
You've lifted
        our sinful load.

A long time ago,
        in Bethlehem
The blessed baby
        was born.
Bringing salvation
        to all men,
So now we never
        walk alone.

Sometimes we let cares
        trouble us so,
Sometimes we worry
        and fret.
Jesus always
        loves us so.
This one thing,
        never forget,

The old world
        may grow wicked,
Troublesome times
        come and go.
But if we follow
        in His footsteps,
One day to Heaven
        we will go.

CHRISTMAS TIMES

I'M SO GLAD HIS BIRTHDAY CAME

I'm so glad His birthday came,
Glory, hallelujah to His name,
I am so glad His birthday came,
We remember every year the same.

Birthday party—praise His name,
For all the love He gives.
Not too long ago, Jesus came,
Help people by the life He lives,

The battles we face are won.
A star for wise men everywhere,
Seeking the king, Jesus is the one,
Our Messiah, the baby born there

Glory to the King of Kings,
A Saviour for all mankind.
Man has freedom, now He sings,
Love of Jesus, now He'll find.

Gifts we give to loved ones here,
In His love for what He did.
Share kindness everywhere,
New life in God is never hid.

Celebrate Him now, around us here,
His Spirit moves, He loves to share.
Joy and peace for all everywhere,
Everyday there's more love to spare.

FACING THE FUTURE

JESUS BIRTHDAY CAME

There was a little Baby Child,
> was born so meek and mild,
Not so long ago,
> not so far away.
Born to show the way
> on that first Christmas day,
Jesus birthday came,
> blessed be His name.

I want to tell the world,
> that Jesus Christ was born,
To save us all from sin,
> on that first Christmas morn.
Now our pathway through life,
> can be free from all strife,
While we walk with Him,
> He is our Christ.

Long before man was born
> God knew the day would come,
He'd have to give His son,
> as the chosen one.
Jesus willingly obeyed,
> and was in a manger laid
Jesus birthday came,
> blessed be His name.

A bright star in the sky—
> a sign to not deny—
Showed wise men the place,
> to find the Baby King.
In the stable where He lay,
> on that first Christmas day,
Jesus birthday came;
> blessed be His name.

CHRISTMAS TIMES

LET'S SING OF CHRISTMAS

If I could sing a song, about Christmas time,
A little song, a little rhyme.
I'd sing of love, and peace on earth,
Of angel's song, the shepherds heard.

If we would sing a song—a Christmas song—
And everyone would sing along,
We would sing of prayer, and brotherhood,
Of everyone trying to do good.

So let's sing a song—a Christmas song—
Come on everyone, now sing along.
A little baby was born on Christmas day,
Help all men; bring peace their way.

In this darkness, see the light,
The newborn King, born this night.
Nevermore lost, and astray,
"Good will to all," the angels say.

We live here now, at home or play,
While there's light, to show the way.
Seek tomorrow, with hope for everyone,
Ch;ristmas joy, through God's chosen Son.

FACING THE FUTURE

OUR CHRISTMAS LOVE

Sitting around the open fire,
Reminiscing over the past year.
Realizing time went so fast,
Spent in sadness or in cheer?

Rain kept things growing,
Each drop from the sky.
Roots drank from its bounty,
They would fade, by and by.

Flowers bloom in the sunshine,
Faded now, for a while.
We enjoy the Winter's fun,
They'll return again in style.

Tomorrow once more we'll be,
Enjoying each other, for a time.
The old cold North wind blows,
Our love will still be fine.

Snowflakes we see falling,
Lie so still on the ground.
Love came together this time,
For Christmas all around.

Love like a flower grows,
Sometimes fades, for a while.
Through wintertime it goes,
Returns again, with a smile.

CHRISTMAS TIMES

OUR SAVIOUR'S BIRTHDAY

In a town called Bethlehem
Not so very long ago,
There was born a baby boy,
Prophets told us so.
He was sent into this world,
From His home above,
The Saviour of mankind,
Save us by His love.

Jesus our Saviour,
Through Mary was conceived,
By the Holy Spirit's power,
For all men to believe.
Reincarnation of God,
To us mere mortal men,
All people everywhere,
Can now enter in.

Many have already chosen,
Jesus as their Lord,
He still is the Saviour,
Lifting sin's heavy load.
He was born in a stable,
That first Christmas day,
For all mankind He came,
To earth a ransom pay.

Remember when you celebrate,
This joyous holiday,
It's not just for the fun,
But our Saviour's birthday.
If you haven't accepted,
This Jesus as your own,
Open to Him there's still time,
He's willing to take us home.

FACING THE FUTURE

MORE ABOUT GOD'S POWER

MORE ABOUT GOD'S POWER

FACING THE FUTURE

GOD MAKES US ABLE

In life, some things are too hard for man.
Then God reaches down, with His mighty hand.
Giving strength, helping us to overcome it all.
Making us able to stand, even after we fall.

We may think sometimes, He doesn't really see.
Wondering if God really cares for me.
Maybe it's just another testing time at hand.
God can make us able to rejoice in the land.

No difference, how dark maybe the night.
He will be there, with the guiding light.
Giving courage to stand, steadfast and sure.
Moving a little closer to Heaven's open door,

I know God is able, for the Bible tells me so.
God is able—gives eternal life to show.
I may never see, all God can do for me.
Till one day in Heaven, for all eternity.

Ask Him; He knows; Blesses them that seek.
God's always ready, caring for the meek.
This world closes in; temptations abound.
Call on His Name—a best friend is found.

He's ever present, for the strong or weak.
Call out in trouble, when you want to speak.
Someone to talk to, a friend who's always there.
He's bigger than life, fame or fortune.

MORE ABOUT GOD'S POWER

GOD'S EYES

When you're hurt, the thoughts ponder,
Exert Your healing power now, Father
Your eyes see from here to yonder,
Recreate! You know just how?

God is walking to and fro,
Through this world we live in.
Beholding man on the go,
Living for self or for Him.

We behold God's creation,
He gives freedom and control.
Do we choose hesitation
Or His way, and save our soul?

A loving Father, reaching out,
Heal their mind and body too.
Victory—what it's all about,
A home for us beyond the blue.

As children He sees where we go,
Closer to Him or farther away.
Precious love, His desire, we know,
In this family, we want to stay.

God is watching, a good father is He,
Through good times and bad.
Good or evil—He can always see,
Our response, after the love we've had.

Do we acknowledge Him there or flee,
With confidence, or in retreat.
He is waiting to set us free,
Till that time, sin we must defeat.

FACING THE FUTURE

HEALING

Power to bind or loose in Jesus name

Faith is substance and evidence,
Giving thanks before we see.
Speak Jesus name in confidence,
To all disease or infirmity,

Is God glorified in your life?
Do you count dying for Christ gain?
Job was righteous—still had strife,
Live for Christ, even through the pain?

Are we ready for deliverance?
Would we go, happy and free?
Return, knowing the relevance?
Worship at His feet, and happy to be.

Do we see our eternal home?
Jesus promised, if we receive.
Eternity nevermore alone,
Redemption's plan, if we believe.

On that hill at Calvary,
Where the Lamb of God was slain.
For all mankind to have victory,
Deliverance and healing, in Jesus name.

MORE ABOUT GOD'S POWER

INFINITELY SECURE

When you may feel all hope is gone,
That's the time His armies are strong.
Strength to climb the highest mountain,
Make our way, to drink at the fountain

The storms of life may knock you around,
We must still try to hold our ground.
Then it happens, when all seems lost,
Along comes Jesus, who paid the cost.

He said, "Lift your hands and praise His name,
Say, "Hallelujah!" since Jesus came.
We can dance for joy, shout to the Lord,
Lift up our hands to the one we adored.

All our burdens try to weigh us down,
Remember His Spirit is still around.
If we heed His call, on our knees we fall,
Cares and troubles—He'll take them all.

Situations come and the thunder may roll,
With God as our helper, He cares for the soul.
Will help every time we need to be free,
Saving, making us people of liberty.

FACING THE FUTURE

IT'S A LONG JOURNEY

It's a long journey, we humans travel on.
Mountains and valleys, from dusk till dawn.
Do we see the troubles? escape from harm?
There's a new day coming—still no alarm.

We must love each other, always being kind.
Reach out to our neighbour, even help the blind.
God made the sunshine, for us all to share.
Put within our hearts, a special place to care.

Some days we need rain, helping things grow.
With the needed moisture falling here below.
Then we see the rainbow—His love is everywhere.
Our home is built on love and very special care.

Each day let us journey, knowing all the time.
We can help each other work things out, so fine.
Just a word for mercy, and wisdom from above.
The creator knows; He'll send down some love.

There's coming a tomorrow; we all will be there.
With the past behind us, the burden that we bear.
Truth is never ending; we'll always want to find.
Like a friend, we hold close, through all of time

Along this road there're flowers—stop and enjoy.
They're helping the beauty, wanting to employ.
Still onward we must journey, all of mankind,
Another step, another mile, new life we'll find.

MORE ABOUT GOD'S POWER

JESUS LORD AND SAVIOUR

We can all serve the same Lord,
We may all carry the same load,
We must bear our cross each day,
Live for Christ and be OK.

He loves us all, died on a cross.
Paid the price to save from loss.
We'll thank Him soon, for what He's done.
This love we feel, is from God's Son.

Alive in Heaven, forever we'll dwell
Living with Jesus who we know so well.
He saves all man, sets him free.
Lives with Him, through eternity.

There are things, that we could say,
Living for Jesus, each passing day.
Forever is a long time, we can tell,
Living in that land, with God to dwell.

FACING THE FUTURE

MORE ABOUT GOD'S POWER

JEHOVAH

I stood all alone, one day, on the shore,
To hear the waves of the sea, as they roar.
Watched the surf pitch, their peaks to the sky,
Wading in the ocean, as the sea rushed by.

Let your ocean rush over me Jehovah,
Jehovah Jireth—the Lord will provide,
Jehovah Nissi—the Lord my banner,
Jehovah Shalom—the Lord send peace,

Jehovah Shammoth—the Lord is there,
Jehovah Tsidkenu—the Lord our righteousness.
Let Your water cleanse and set me free,
You give all things, for eternity.

Waters filled with what Heaven brings,
Surrounded by the love, of the King of Kings.
Cleansed by the blood of the lamb, sanctified.
My Lord and my God, You keep us satisfied.

With Jesus I'm walking, day by day,
Our Lord and Saviour helps in every way.
Keep us from sinning, on our journey home,
To our mansion in glory, never alone.

FACING THE FUTURE

JONAH

Get back Jonah! Don't you see,
Can't go sailing, out on the sea.
Should be preaching, in Nineveh,
Not running away, from God's law.

Into the belly of the big fish,
Who is looking for you in a dish,
Should have listened to God's call,
Moved with Him—not run and fall.

You've still got decisions to make,
What's it going to be, will you break?
Will you listen, to the Master's call?
Will you be set free, or run and fall?

There's a big storm, coming your way,
Hear the high winds blow, feel them sway,
Waves crashing; ship's starting to sink,
We'll all be lost souls, cast into the brink.

Among us, one's hiding—shouldn't be here,
Away from God's will—should be there,
Doing the task that he was called to do,
Into the water, we'll pull through.

Jonah cried, "It is I, who ran from the call,
Throw me in the water, it will settle it all,
Should have followed God, now here I am,
God is love—you can't run from His plan."

Soon we'll find there's a Master plan,
The journey should lead, to Heaven's land.
A big fish swallowed Jonah, then up on dry ground,
If we follow Jesus, we'll also be found.

MORE ABOUT GOD'S POWER

MASTER AND SAVIOUR

Jesus is my Lord, my Master and Saviour,
Jesus is my Lord, my Master and Saviour,
Jesus is my Lord, my Master and Saviour,
Now and forever, glory, to His name.

Praise you God, for the Blood of the lamb,
King of Kings, Lord of Lords, and the great I AM.
God of old, hallelujah, and God of the now,
King forever, and through, eternity.

Jesus is the one, who delivers me daily,
Jesus is the one, who delivers me daily,
Jesus is the one, who delivers me daily,
From sin, Hallelujah, and from shame.

Let the peace of Christ, rule in your heart,
Let the peace of Christ, reign in your heart.
And whatever you do, in word or deed,
Do it all, in the name, of the Lord.

Give Him thanks, give Him thanks,
To God, through Christ our Lord.
Give Him thanks, give Him thanks,
To God, through Christ our Lord.

FACING THE FUTURE

PLANTING OF THE LORD

It fell by the wayside—fell by the wayside, Lord,
Trodden down, fowls of the air ate it up, oh Lord.
Help me make this soil more fertile,
Work it, 'till Your seeds will grow, oh Lord,
Life fruitful; Your seeds growing everywhere.

The sower went out—the sower went out to sow,
His seed was scattered, everywhere we know.
Seeking ground that's ready and worked up,
Waiting for the planting of the Lord.
When He comes will He find us, living in His Word?

Some fell on a rock—hard old rocky soil oh Lord,
Lacking moisture, withered away, oh Lord.
Help me make this soil more fertile, oh Lord,
Work it 'till Your seeds will grow, oh Lord,
Life fruitful; Your seeds growing everywhere.

Some seed fell among thorns—thorny ground,
Thorns sprang up, choked the plants, oh Lord,
Make this soil more fertile, oh Lord,
Work it 'till Your seeds will grow, oh Lord,
Life fruitful, Your seeds growing everywhere.

Some fell upon good ground—good fertile ground,
Sprang up; bear fruit, a hundred fold, oh Lord.
Make this soil more fertile, oh Lord,
Work it 'till Your seeds will grow, oh Lord,
Life fruitful; Your seeds growing everywhere.

MORE ABOUT GOD'S POWER

POOL OF BETHESDA

Resting by the Pool of Bethesda,
Many years, there all alone.
Where the healing waters are flowing,
God sends healings from the throne.

Every day I've suffered with pain and sickness,
Oh the vexation it brings to my soul.
My hope rests completely on Jesus,
Believe, and let Him have full control.

That I may do what is right and pleasing,
For you to see my need, and intervene.
On my behalf and those who are trusting,
Waiting for the healing water stream.

Like John, banished on the Isle of Patmos,
Hard labour—imprisoned for belief in God.
The angel helped, gave revelation,
In the Spirit, he spoke words that will prod.

Servants sent forth from God's throne,
Angels for those who seek God's face.
In life's journey, there is so much power,
We'd never make it without God's help.

When we're down, walking through darkness,
It seems all the light has completely gone,
Know He'll help, if we call on Him, believing,
He loves us so; He'll send angels to help.

FACING THE FUTURE

SHOUT AND CELEBRATE

Worship and praise to our God,
Wind fills the place—we know it's Him.

Praise to God and His Holy Presence,
We've got the victory deep within.

No limitations what God will do,
His ability unlimited—victory over strife.

In Him we feel a Father's loving touch,
He's the way through everything in life.

This world needs Jesus, to see their way,
Shining through the dark of night.

With our hand in His, everyday
Our path we see, with His light.

Let's praise Him now, Lord and King,
Give Him your love—rejoice and sing.

He'll be with us here and eternally,
There're no needs—Jesus is everything.

Shout and celebrate—victory is here,
We welcome You, God, to our shore.

Perform Your mighty work in me,
Save and deliver forevermore.

MORE ABOUT GOD'S POWER

THE ANOINTING OIL

Let me touch the hem of Your garment, Lord.
Where the oil of anointing flows.
Oh Lord let me feel the power of Your touch.
My needs are so great, I know.

Just to be there, in Your presence.
At Your feet, humbly I wait.
To see the love, and feel Your kindness.
We're friends—it's never to late.

The weakness of flesh struggling on.
Towards new life in Your home.
Tomorrows will be with You forever.
Family gathered—no one alone.

I knocked at the door for Your blessing.
Your great love, all around, everywhere.
Now I see You're ever present,
If we knock, You always care.

Seeking, yet not seen with these eyes.
You're still there, wonders to perform.
Through faith, I'll wait for the answer.
It's all in Your time—we're never alone.

I seek for You, and need an answer.
Deliver me from this trouble I'm in.
Every day, I seek Your presence.
Since You saved me from sin.

FACING THE FUTURE

THIRTY THREE BIRTHDAYS

Just a little baby, born of a virgin in Bethlehem,
Prophecies of old, about His coming foretold.
In a manger lay, on that first birthday,
Christ was born; man would never walk alone.
Next in this journey, a couple birthdays went by,
In another place, away from His hometown.
King Herod sought His life,
Bringing death and strife,
The angel warned,
Go to another land—escape danger.
Soon the time has moved along,
Next we sing the birthday song,
Back in the homeland, the place of His birth.
Joseph warned in a dream,
Flee from the king's evil scheme,
Went to Nazareth as the prophecy calls Him a Nazarene.
Then a few more years slip by,
They shout the birthday cry,
Living a pleasant life, working the carpenter's trade.
Destiny led Him on,
Teaching at twelve, in the church throng,
No longer a child.
He obtained the Master's call.
Baptized by John, while the people watched on,
His miracles and ministry increased day by day.
Tempted by Satan in the wilderness,
Gaining freedom from that stress,
We who believe, can live the same life too.

MORE ABOUT GOD'S POWER

THIRTY THREE BIRTHDAYS (PART B)

Birthdays pass by each year,
Every one made His message clear,
Glorifying God our Creator from on high.
As John in the River Jordan,
Met the Master on His mission,
Baptizing Him, Heaven opened and God spoke.
The Spirit of God, descended like a dove,
Lighting upon Jesus, God's only Son.
A voice from Heaven said,
"This is my beloved Son,
Whom I love; and with Him I am well pleased."
Anointed for His ministry,
No more mention about birthday,
Still led by God
He was consumed by the mission at hand.
Everywhere doing good,
Saving souls as He could,
Destination calls,
He'll be the Lamb who was slain.
Thirty-three birthdays—the final year of our Lord,
To live among us down here in the flesh.
Next we'll see Him on high,
When He returns in the sky,
To take His children to their new home forevermore.
Now every year we celebrate,
Please don't hesitate,
To remember the birthday of our Saviour and king,
Just thirty-three birthdays,
Of a man who lives always,
Interceding for these trials we must go through.

FACING THE FUTURE

THE POWER OF GOD

Sometimes we stop and wonder,
About things we do and say.
Never knowing, in these little things,
God has His own way.

The power of God is unlimited,
His power is so divine.
He keeps His hand upon us,
To guide us, through all time.

There are questions about creation,
There are doubts and lies, that's true,
If we believe alone in God,
We'll see the way through.

How somebody could make the stars,
Shape the world, just as we see it today!
God's power is so unlimited,
It was meant to be just this way.

The power of God made us people,
With the plan, we serve Him.
Given a free will, many disobey Him,
Walk the lonely roads of sin.

One day soon we will see Him,
Through the clouds in the sky.
All men will be able to see Him,
The saved go to a home in the sky.

MORE ABOUT GOD'S POWER

THY WILL OH LORD

I have no other
    life to live,
Passing through
    this world below.
Jesus came to earth,
    a ransom to give,
That all mankind
    may know.

God gives to man
    understanding,
About life
    and Heaven above.
Sin came,
    and death it was handing,
Seek God, He'll save us
    through His love.

God's will is given,
    if we will ask,
Show us the way
    to our heavenly home.
Follow His ways
    is our earthly task,
He'll stay close—
    never leave us alone.

We seek and trust
    forever in God,
He's our sufficiency
    for every need.
Now we flee from sin
    on this sod,
Saving message;
    His Word, we heed.

FACING THE FUTURE

TO BE BLESSED

Wrestling with the angel, a blessing we seek,
Messenger from God, to those who are meek.
Here on a mission, we stand and receive,
From the hands of our God—we must believe.

Understand the power, to be blessed with God,
All things He made, below on this sod,
So greet the stranger, pursue patience,
Our blessings are waiting, in His presence.

So gentle, so precious, the love, of God,
Care for His children, on this path we trod,
Reality beckons; giving all the way,
Pursue His presence, forever, OK.

Even Jacob, a mortal, empowered by God,
Blessing His life, on the path He trod,
Endured the struggle, an angel to face,
We too must seek Him to win in life's race.

We can see it coming, down from above,
Somewhere there's a message, sent in love,
Seek and continue, in His words we will see,
A blessing for all men, part of destiny.

MORE ABOUT GOD'S POWER

AN EAGLE

Like an eagle,
Don't fall.
Carefully learn how to fly,
Up and out of the nest.
Soar through the heavens,
Through the open skies.
The cool, gentle breezes blowing,
Soaring like eagles, through it all.
There may be danger, in the darkness,
Keep on seeking,
Spread your wings.
Look to the sky through the dark,
Speed your flight to Father's arms.
Through the clouds,
You'll see Him coming,
He'll help through trouble,
Keep you strong.
From the nest, to this flight,
Now you'll be in His plans forevermore.
The time is ready,
You must prepare for the Master's love.
Parting troubles, and into clear skies,
Trusting by faith,
Like eagles you'll fly.
Our life is in God's hands,
Just like the eagle,
We soar in Him.
Not of this earth anymore,
Now we are His and in His plan
Through the heavens we soar.

FACING THE FUTURE

DON'T STOP HOPING

Keep on holding to the Master's hand.
Through the storms of life, He'll come.
Hope in God; all things will pass.
He'll be there, to help us stand.

Don't stop hoping—it won't be long.
So many trials, and battles come.
With Jesus, we journey, day by day.
One day we'll stand before His throne.

Weary pilgrims, you're feeling alone.
So many trials, and battles come.
With Jesus we journey, day by day,
One day we'll stand before His throne.

We're going to praise Him, standing true.
Holding His hand, all day through.
Hoping, always, our Master will come.
He's making that home, beyond the blue.

We look back, to where we've been.
All the struggles—dealing with sin.
Then the beauty of salvation is seen.
Through the ages, with the angels we'll sing.

MORE ABOUT GOD'S POWER

GOD

He is big enough to use earth as His footstool,
Powerful enough to speak stars into existence.
The sun, moon, all planets He placed there,
The sun the greater light, the moon the lesser.
Placed stars in the sky to be lights in the night,
Created the earth for man, and made man for it.
Created systems that make our planet habitable,
Filled this earth with all the animals needed.
Powers of creation, in wild form, as tornados,
Hurricanes, cyclones, earthquakes, volcanoes.
Such power loosed on earth from time of creation,
Still Jesus, God's Son, speaks and calms the storm.
God the creator can form the mountains,
Give strength for us to move the mountains.
God stilled the troubled water in the beginning,
Jesus stilled troubled waters in Galilee.
There isn't anything that God cannot do,
We must believe and ask Him for an intervention.
As mere human beings, we are fragile and weak,
His power is unlimited, He hears us when we pray.
Just depend on His ever unfailing arms of grace,
God is love, all who know Him have this same love.
He made a way for us to live eternally with Him,
Just pray and believe, confessing the Word of God.
If any man believe in His heart the Lord Jesus,
And confess with His mouth, God raised Him from the dead,
He is saved—He is a new creation,
We are brand new—justified—just as if we never sinned.
Then God prepares us to be a sanctuary for Him,
To come and dwell, setting up habitation within,
And we together lifting up the name of Jesus,
For all mankind to see His love now and forevermore.

FACING THE FUTURE

GOD IS THE ONE

God is the one,
Who made the mountains.
He created the wind.
His thoughts known to man.

He changes day into night,
Rules over all the earth.
This is His Name,
The Lord God Almighty.

The Lord made the stars,
That shine in heavenly light.
He turns darkness into light,
And day into night.

He calls the waters of the seas,
And pours them out on the earth.
His name is the Lord.
He brings down strongholds.

You may not understand,
Why things happen to all.
From now to the sweet bye and bye,
We as sheep wonder why.

We are young, and now growing older,
He is there all the time.
Even our passion changes, over what?
God sends angels to help on our way.

MORE ABOUT GOD'S POWER

GOD IS WITH US

If any barriers, know God is greater.
If any mountains, know God is greater.

If ever weary, the Lord will help us win.
Any problems? Put your trust in Him,

He'll lead through waters—we can't see the way.
He'll carry all times, when storms toss and sway.

He's the help for all ages—never will He change.
Stand by our side, though life can be strange.

Confide alone in Him, for everything you need.
Standing on His promises, all His words to heed.

Living your life in Him, seeking for His will.
Waiting to hear His voice, consistent and still.

As you walk this road of life, remember Joshua.
Victory over sin and strife, obeying God's law.

He was chosen the leader, to the promised land.
No doubting—just obeying God's command.

One day we'll see them in the presence of our Lord.
All saints who love Him: our Master we've adored.

With God's children, from the beginning of time.
Forever round God's table, in His love so fine.

FACING THE FUTURE

OUR PAST

OUR PAST

FACING THE FUTURE

ANNIVERSARY IS GOLDEN

Through many years of love, my dear,
Our hearts grow closer still.
Though twilight time is drawing near,
I'll love you, yes I will.

Happy anniversary, till the very end,
Happy anniversary, always to you.
Want you to know, you're my special friend,
Always will be, my dearest one too.

Through these years I'll stand by you,
Try to understand when times get rough.
Hold you close, send flowers too,
It's hard as a friend to do enough.

Together, God blessed our home, dear,
With sweetness, a little family all our own.
Though life passes by with some wear,
The task before us; keep our home.

Someday, when forever we will stand,
In a home we've lived our whole life for.
Will be such happiness, in that land,
Walking hand in hand, through Heaven's door.

OUR PAST

COMING HOME

I've worked on the West Coast, mighty hard,
From factory, to picking fruit, and the old train yard.
Fields to harvest on the Prairies, growing lots of grain,
Still homesick for my roots, coming back home again.

Coming home again, I'm coming home again,
Where the sea gulls call, speak my name.
Coming home again, coming home to stay,
The special little place, by the waters sway.

Worked through central Canada, with all the beauty there,
High rise cities stretch for miles—shipping everywhere.
Take me to the country, with lots of room to roam,
Coming back to my Island, treasure, down home.

No matter where you live from the East Coast to the West,
This land so full of splendour, God's handiwork at it's best.
I live on a special Island; it's where I belong,
A little garden paradise, singing a happy song.

FACING THE FUTURE

OUR PAST

HOMELAND

The stars shine brighter,
Over this little island home.
The moon shines its light,
where we're never alone.
We'll walk here in freedom,
With care for each one.
Thank God for creation,
A gold nugget we've won.

It's our home we love,
God keeps it safe and true.
Our children can run and play,
Enjoy the skies so blue.
Neighbours help each other,
When we need an extra hand.
Time passes; we enjoy life,
Loving our dear homeland.

Day by day we work and labour,
Toil and sweat—each woman and man.
Tells the tale of survival,
Our families had a plan.
In the mornings, work in daylight,
Others toil, in shifts as well.
Endure throughout the seasons,
Times change, the truth will tell.

FACING THE FUTURE

IF YOU CROSS THE RIVER

If you cross over the river before I go,
Look for my dad; tell him we miss him so.
Walk with him in glory on streets so fair,
Tell him soon we're coming, God's love to share.
Watch the stars as they twinkle in God's big sky,
Sending a message from the sweet by and by.
For us who still labour in this world below,
Waiting for our turn, when it's our time to go.
We look at the flowers, and the trees on this ground,
Everything has its season—its true, we have found.
The beauty of the sky, the clouds, that water the ground,
Gives life for the harvest—it's true we have found.
Maybe you've lost a loved one, a mother or a dad,
Sometimes leaving comes too early, making us feel sad.
We know over there with Jesus, in that land so fair,
In a new land called Glory, where His love we'll share.
By the river side, in the still of the day,
I saw the light shine—such a beautiful array.
I saw a double rainbow, stretched from shore to shore.
It seemed like God's love, we feel o'er and o'er
There I stood in silence, to absorb it in my mind,
Words raced through my thoughts, about life sublime,
Even though we've parted for a while, here below,
One day—forever in that land, we will part no more.

OUR PAST

ON A RAILWAY HEADING HOME

Just place me on that old train track,
Get on board, with your things in a sack.
Place me on that old railway track,
I'm leaving here, and not coming back.

I see the sunshine, and it's sinking low,
Was up and shining—now it's time to go.
See that sun leave the sky, sinking down so low,
Lord, help me now; I don't know where to go.

They tell me, Lord, you were placed on a tree,
They say you died to set us free.
I see the grass so green over the hill,
Will my soul find rest, trusting at will?

I've seen things grow so free and new,
Love comes and leaves us to work it through.
This heart of mine seems burdened down,
I'll get on that train—pull out of this town.

In wings of flight, I'll fly away home,
The land where no one will be alone.
Peace and love, shared forevermore,
Looking for a stop on that golden shore.

FACING THE FUTURE

OUR PAST

LIFE MAY BE ROUGH

Life may sometimes be very rough,
Times we're living in may get tough,
You have to express what's on your mind,
Try to be good and never, never, unkind.

My mom she told me when I was a lad,
"You know you should be good, never, bad.
Live your life, remember God's golden rule,
Do your part and you'll be nobody's fool."

I love the day, when the sun is shining bright,
Also the starry sky, and moonlit night.
A wife and a family, standing by,
With them I know, God's care doesn't lie.

Leaving home makes you feel bad,
Everywhere you go, it's nice to be glad.
Try to be smooth, and gentle with everyone,
Don't mistreat at all—your time might come.

Storms come, and pass by in time,
Prepare to survive them, with all mankind.
Provide help to all who stands in need,
Live for truth, and always pay heed.

FACING THE FUTURE

OUR PAST

SEEDS YOU SOW

Yes! I know God loves country people,
He loves city people to.
Together down these same old highways,
Remembering God's golden rule.

I thank God for all those country roads,
Where I used to walk, when but a lad.
Whatever seed you sow, you'll have to grow,
And reap the harvest someday.

Just to hear Dad singing "Lily Of The Valley,"
How those songs rang across my mind.
Mother reading from the good old Bible,
About all those promises so divine.

God blessed this family to be a shelter for me,
A strong tower to live in, day and night.
Storms of life beat upon the walls,
Still they withstood the winds, all right.

My heart cries out! thanks for all the memories,
Running like a river all the way back to you.
My longing—desire—for those peaceful country roads.
I need to never forget what I've been through.

FACING THE FUTURE

RELATIONSHIPS

RELATIONSHIPS

FACING THE FUTURE

A LIFE'S MISSION

A Creator, so awesome, made all things in time,
Stars, moon, sun, all the planets in line.
Like a clock, intricately ticking so fine,
We're here in creation—display of God's mind.

The sun will set; the moon will rise,
Stars and clouds always fill the skies.
Will we search for truth or fall for lies?
God, Creator of all things—even time that flies.

We each have a mission—live, work, and dream—
Compelled to fit in this worldwide scene.
Today, tomorrow, we'll be part of the team,
Work for survival in life's stormy stream.

All our lives are recorded, on pages of time,
Like the weather system: did we live fine?
Or is it just like the wind, blowing in line?
We live and breathe—all part of mankind.

Life seems so fast—getting harder to stand,
Yet what other choices do we have as mere men?
Open your eyes; look across this great land,
We're part of creation, trying to understand.

RELATIONSHIPS

A LITTLE CHILD'S FAITH

Yes I believe in Jesus,
He saved my weary soul,
Took everything—made it new,
Took my sin—made me whole.
Accept Him like a little child,
Believe, trusting in His name.
Oh! Lord, come and save me,
I'm overjoyed that He came.

Jesus changed everything,
Made it brand new again.
Once I was just a baby,
Not sure of life's gain.
Finding life's contentment,
In just food, rest, and drink.
Then I came to Jesus,
He gave new thoughts to think

Jesus is my Father,
He's my Brother too.
Fill your heart like a Mother,
Love like a Sister to.
So if we're ever discouraged,
Sad, lonely, or blue,
I know Someone who'll be there,
To show just what to do.

I turn to Jesus with the faith,
Just like a little child.
Believe in Him alone,
He will safely guide.
Show the kingdom of His Father,
Not only meat or drink,
Righteous, peace and joy,
Pull us back from the brink.

FACING THE FUTURE

HOLD ON

Well I put my soul in the hands of my Saviour,
Don't have to worry any more.
I put my soul in the hands of my Saviour,
He's opened Heaven's door.
The sun is shining every morning, I know,
Down in this heart of mine.
Since Jesus came along,
Now He's a good friend of mine.

He died upon the tree at Calvary,
To wash me white as snow.
When sometimes I fall in sin,
I know just where to go.
By the grace of God He washes away,
Every sin I make.
If I believe in Him alone,
He all my burdens takes.

The Devil may come along sometimes,
Trying to tempt my soul.
But by the grace of the living Saviour,
He has made me whole.
Get behind me you old Devil,
Satan you'll have to flee.
Cause I'm going all the way with Jesus,
Now, and throughout eternity.

Though sometimes I may be in the valley,
That's all right, you know.
Just like a plant, every Christian,
Has times when they got to grow.
You must let your light shine so bright,
Chasing darkness away.
So happiness, love, peace, and joy,
Will come here to stay.

RELATIONSHIPS

JUST A PRODIGAL SON

Once I walked, the pathway of sin,
Finding such discouragement within.

Until one day, Jesus rescued me,
Now I'll live with Him, eternally.

Just a prodigal son, walking all alone,
With no secure hold, on my eternal home.

Didn't know God's Son, who was crucified,
I was lost and running, trying to hide.

Something missing that couldn't be bought,
God's love and care, that's what I forgot.

Now turn around to Jesus, don't hesitate,
The time for man's salvation is getting late.

Just a prodigal son, alone, with nothing more,
A promise of standing, on Heaven's shore.

When all the trials on earth have been won,
Enter that land—Jesus is the sun.

People of this world have a choice to make,
Turn to God and live, for Heaven's sake.

Do we care enough, where we'll spend eternity?
Choose now and live, the life clear to see.

FACING THE FUTURE

ON THE SEA OF LIFE

We've been sailing many years,
O'er this sea of life,
Somewhere in the distance,
A land free from strife,

A mountain in the distance,
High, yet still we'll climb.
It's the shore of destiny,
New beginning for mankind.

Over there in the distance,
We'll know it's all worthwhile.
Every trial—every heartache,
Every tear and every smile.

I keep looking and I see it,
This promise that we need.
A new land of opportunity,
Gives us a chance to be free.

RELATIONSHIPS

OVERCOMERS

"Be not overcome with evil,
Overcome evil with good.,"
This spoke the Lord to all men,
Overcome evil with good.

On this path we travel,
Two main choices to make.
Jesus as Lord, on one hand,
The other, evil may take.

We are but a clay form,
Inside this temple, we dwell.
Walking this pathway, as all men,
God's love—His stories we tell.

Many desires on my heart,
Seek God's will first.
We must always, do our part,
For living water we thirst.

Are you an overcomer for Jesus?
Are you over coming for Him?
Do you keep hope, inside always?
To be an overcomer and win.

In this life time moves along,
Journey from darkness to light.
Profit comes in redemption's song,
Through our troubles, doing right

FACING THE FUTURE

WRITING FOR A FUTURE

WRITING FOR A FUTURE

FACING THE FUTURE

FRESH

Fresh every morning,
Yesterday? Yesterday?
Tomorrow is in His hands,
Renewed in Christ.
On this pilgrim way,
It is we who decide,
How far our faith will reach.
If we can hold on long enough,
To really, really, believe,
For now and for always.

Kindness even through darkness,
Everywhere all around,
Light of God shines through it all,
Even from Calvary's hill.
What degree of intimacy,
To have with Jesus,
Priority means we care.
My soul thirsts for you,
True intimacy,
Will last forevermore.

In pursuit of a dream,
Longing deep within,
The passion drives strong,
Through all the living hours.
No night or day between,
The reality of this Heaven,
Can we ever seek more than this.
Stirred by conscience,
In God we trust always,
Truth is fresh with no defeat.

HOW FAR IS HEAVEN?

It happened one cold autumn;
        leaves began to fall,
We lost our Dad.
        He heard the Master call.
A light now is shining,
        on streets of glory land,
My dad—the angels took Him,
        in the Master's plan.

The leaves change colour,
        so beautiful too see,
Soon they end their season;
        they are set free.
Like all things on earth—
        live, grow and die,
We came as a baby;
        soon it's time to say goodbye.

Life's so brief—must be more
        then what we can see,
Money, fame, all those things,
        like living happily.
Hear Him warn,
        we'll soon be leaving here,
Our chariot's ready—
        home to our Saviour dear.

Life's journeys can be
        full of troubles and pain,
Stormy waters we travel,
        in loss or gain.
Let Jesus show the way,
        in the daytime or night,
He shows the path of all,
        both wrong or right.

FACING THE FUTURE

IS EVERYTHING REALLY EVERYTHING?

The things I desire—need every day
Like food and shelter, a job with pay.
Some parts of life bring uncertainty,
Wonder why these things also must be?

We ask the Father, for sunshine or rain,
Sometimes it comes, or we just try again.
Requests we've made, pass with time,
Reasons are infinitely over our mind.

It's a matter of heart—desires we show
Our Master whispers, soft and low
What we need is Him, above everything
Relationship sweet, He is our King.

Deception can come, convincing us so,
To buy or to try, some things as we know.
The truth remains, consistent as rain
Seek the source, from where it came.

Again, we can know eternity's plan,
Getting to hold the Master's hand.
All tomorrows in peace—made by Him,
Live in that mansion, saved from all sin.

See the future; roses never fade,
Peace forever—debts have been paid.
Love of the Master, given to all,
If we believe, and answer His call.

WRITING FOR A FUTURE

LIGHT OF LOVE

Help the lighthouse shine brighter,
Help the lighthouse shine further,
Lord shine Your light,
All around us here.

In a world with lots of darkness,
Help Your lighthouse shine on us,
Thanks, dear Lord,
For Your Word to show the way.

He said He'll meet us on the mountain,
So we look to Him and pray.
The Lord helps us through the darkness,
Be ready if He calls today.

In this world the time is passing,
Full of struggle and woe.
Let the light of His love shine through,
Then to Heaven we're going to go.

Drink from Your fountain every day,
Stay close by Your side all the way.
Ready to share Your love everywhere,
Knowing You're our Father, and we love You dear.

There were ten virgins gathered,
To the wedding with the groom.
Then the call came, "Go to meet Him,"
You know He's coming soon.

Five had lamps trimmed and ready,
The other five—He came too soon.
Jesus, the bridegroom, is coming,
In your heart, does He have room?

FACING THE FUTURE

TIME OR A MIRACLE

When you believe in your heart,
God can do all things.
Trained from a very young age,
"Everything works together for good,
To them that love God."
You always expect your needs in life,
To always be taken care of,
Because you believe in God,
And confess in His Holy Name.
God as a Good Father.
How could there ever be,
An area of lack or neglect?
Like everything else in life,
There is always the other side,
Of the story, as we live it—
There goes another day.
Maybe you looked for success.
Maybe a job with sufficiency.
Where you could take control,
Of your life and its demands.
See all the bills paid,
With no problems unresolved.
The provisions all taken care of.
Even something put away for tomorrow,
In case of an emergency.
You're left hoping, and it came true.
Still there comes the sun rising again.
Before you know it,
The day has been spent,
It's night time and dark again.

NIGHT POEMS

NIGHT POEMS

FACING THE FUTURE

A PLACE OF REFUGE

Consider the birds, they have a place to rest.
He made the trees for them to call home.
He'll prepare for those who pursue the test.
A place with Him—never alone.

Even when times of trouble may come,
"Flee like a bird to your mountain."
There may be danger you must flee from.
He's made a place close to the fountain.

"Wait on the Lord renew your strength,
Mount up on wings like eagles,
Run and not grow weary, walk and not faint
Teach me Lord, teach me Lord, to wait".

NIGHT POEMS

PERFECTED IN HIM

Good morning Jesus!
    Please help and guide me.
Through this path—
    I'd love Your company.
In this world,
    there's so much damage.
I see in You, beauty,
    and ability to change

All our perfection,
    is in Christ our Lord.
In our life, You've helped
    along this road.
You were there,
    each and every trial.
Helping us walk;
    every foot; every mile.

In the morning,
    the sun will rise
We see it shine,
    with no disguise.
In life, there's mountains,
    we've got to climb.
Surviving—not forgetting
    what we left behind.

Christmas time we remember,
    Jesus' birthday.
He came to save all man
    gone astray.
If we believe the price
    paid at Calvary.
Confessing to God,
    then being set free.

FACING THE FUTURE

SOOTHING WATERS

So lift your heart and lift your hands,
Give praises to His Holy Name.
For God is God, and God is great,
He always is the same.

He loved us then; He loves us now,
He'll make a home on high.
He makes a way—a path through life—
In the sweet by and by.

He's King Of Kings, the great I AM,
For now and evermore.
If we will only trust in Him,
Satisfied till Heaven's shore.

He gives mankind all His love,
As a loving father would do.
A helping hand all through life,
Even dark and stormy too.

Even when hope sometimes seems gone,
He's there, and will always care.
The storms may blow, and tempest toss,
He speaks with love to share.

NIGHT POEMS

THE WIND BLOWS

The wind blows,
        it's so revealing,
A power,
        not made by hands,
It is sometimes,
        smooth and gentle,
Sometimes rebels,
        destroys the land.

Whatever reason,
        we're part of creation,
Presentation
        of nature's plan.
Rich or poor—
        we're in it together,
Plan for the future,
        it's in our hands.

The grains and flowers,
        the grass and the land,
The wind in the sails,
        the sea on earth's span.
The wind moves,
        see results so grand,
Like a gigantic structure,
        of a master plan.

The wind is blowing;
        do you hear it speak?
A voice of command,
        not very weak,
This whole creation,
        made for man so meek,
Affects everything,
        even as we seek.

FACING THE FUTURE

WAIT FOR HIM

Waiting for an answer—
    all patience gone.
I know it's there—
    must hold on.
All my strength I use;
    the way is so long.
Darkness closes in;
    doubt comes so strong.

Looking for tomorrow—
    need strength within.
Must gain higher ground—
    never give in.
Sunshine on the mountain—
    a prize to win,
Tomorrows are waiting;
    we must begin.

Desire and passion,
    spent on dreams every day.
Hopes and cares—
    journey on with some dismay.
Climb mountains;
    swim waters, deep and long.
Answers for our struggle,
    like visions in a song.

We see Him beside us—
    there all the time.
In doubting, He was reason—
    fruit from the vine.
Choice words of wisdom,
    it's love, a helping hand.
With You we make it.
    thank you God, now we stand.

NIGHT POEMS

GOD LOVES HIS CHILDREN

Sometimes it takes tears in our eyes,
As we avoid all Satan's lies.
Going on, when the way seems dark,
Staying on the way, close to the mark.

Like a parent watching over their child,
See them avoid things that are wild.
Have some failures, now and then,
Still growing up, to be women and men.

Keep on child! You can do it every time,
He'll be right by your side, standing in line.
His grace is sufficient, all the time,
Showing us the way to avoid lying.

Keep on child! God's love is enough,
To help through life, no matter how tough.
There's always a way, to make it home,
Trusting God and His love—nevermore alone.

Some times through life, mountains seem high,
If we turn from God, wondering why.
Then we lift our eyes—see those loving arms,
Saying, "Come on child, flee from alarms."

FACING THE FUTURE

GOD AND HIS SON

GOD AND HIS SON

FACING THE FUTURE

ALL SELF TO THEE OH LORD

I have felt, sometimes,
    I was being torn apart,
Because of a burden,
    stressed on my heart.
I know there's only
    one way to clear this doubt,
By trusting in Jesus,
    giving cause to shout.

Things happen like a word
    or action done,
Which doesn't
    glorify God's Son.
I know I'm slipping—
    need a helping hand,
I go to Jesus;
    He gives love so grand.

Sometimes things hurt
    this temple I'm in,
Because there's more
    I must give to Him.
Not because He demands it
    to be just so,
It's the reason to Calvary
    Jesus had to go.

So now I'll continue,
    onward in the way,
I need Jesus—
    less of this earth and clay.
One day,
    burdens will be all gone,
To live awaiting,
    that day to dawn.

GOD AND HIS SON

LOVING JESUS

Loving Lord Jesus,
You're all my heart's desire.
I give myself to You,
Fill my soul with Holy Fire.

Jesus, shine so new,
As it was when we first met.
At the cross I laid it down,
One time—I'll never forget.

Flowing in the river,
Filled with Holy Fire.
Your bride is being adorned,
With all our heart's desire.

Wedding garments on,
Vessels filled to the brim.
Awaiting the midnight cry,
We shall be ready to go in.

Feet dance like calves,
Just released from the stalls.
Dancing through the meadows,
As our Saviour calls.

Come like fresh spring rains,
Like water in dessert places.
Cleanse and wash us clean,
Show your Glory on our faces.

FACING THE FUTURE

JESUS

Jesus, Jesus, Jesus,
That's all I want to say.

Jesus, Jesus, Jesus,
Means more and more each day.

Jesus, Saviour, Master,
Always will be for me.

Healer and my Guide,
Through life and eternity.

Jesus, Jesus, Jesus,
The man from Galilee.

Jesus, Jesus, Jesus,
You bring peace to me.

Jesus, Jesus, Jesus,
I'll serve you at any cost.

Jesus, Jesus, Jesus,
You saved my life from loss.

Jesus, Jesus, Jesus,
Prophecy about You came true.

Jesus, Jesus, Jesus,
All the way to Heaven with You.

GOD AND HIS SON

NEVER ALONE

You may have many times in life,
When even love seems forgotten.
We all need someone to lean on,
Believe, and you'll see Him there.

I will never be alone anymore,
Since I started serving Jesus as Lord.
Even humans know He is Divine,
That's why I put all my trust in Him.

In life we must keep going on,
Troubles may also appear.
We understand—but not all things,
The reason I trust Him as friend.

The night seems dark and so hard,
Keep believing in God's Power Divine.
There is coming a far brighter day,
With Jesus as the sun, to always shine

FACING THE FUTURE

HE WAS ON TRIAL

He was on trial for me,
Jesus stood trial for me.
He laid down His life—His own precious life,
My Lord was on trial for me.

Born and moulded in sin,
I had not Jesus living within.
Until one day I finally realized,
He was on trial for me.

Living by God's promises now,
Jesus really can show us how.
Remember, our Lord carried our sinful load,
And was put on trial for you and me.

I had pictured where I would be,
Living in sin through eternity,
Now, by the grace of God, a different path I tread,
With Jesus who stood trial for me.

In this world of toil and snare,
With Jesus, there is love to share.
He stood all alone, to show man the way home,
He was on trial for you and me.

GOD AND HIS SON

THOSE SCARS

Those scars were
    because of me,
I who am
    so unworthy.
Agony and shame,
    You bore on the tree,
Open mine eyes,
    that I may see.

The choice was Yours,
    to go to the cross,
For man
    blinded by sin.
The way of salvation
    for the lost,
Through the blood,
    we can enter in.

You're preparing
    a home for the saved,
For us,
    mere children of clay.
All our lives
    on the altar we've laid.
Jesus is
    the only true way.

I'll keep
    pressing on,
Till time
    lingers no more,
Walk in peace,
    knowing God's Son.
God's promises
    we're waiting for.

FACING THE FUTURE

GOD'S DIVIDENDS

In this world
    I may not have,
Riches, wealth,
    or fame.
Jesus is that
    and so much more,
The reason
    to men He came.

Man was
    made by God,
Out of
    dust and clay.
Not rich—
    just plain sod,
A soul to never
    rust or decay.

The immeasurable cost
    of paving with gold,
On the streets
    of this world below.
Not likely here,
    but in Heaven it's used,
In that city where
    we'll never grow old.

Priceless is the cost
    of a man's soul,
The redemption,
    for all to know.
Leaves us speechless—
    being part of His plan,
Greater love
    can no man show.

GOD AND HIS SON

A FEW DAYS AFTER DEATH

I really don't know for sure,
When my time is up here on earth,
I'm not trying to leave early.
I believe I'm saved,
And Jesus waits for His children
Leaving this body is to be with the Lord,
In His time.
Quite a journey,
From this planet to God's open arms.
Just to know He's waiting—expecting our arrival.
Leave this Old World—into God's presence for all eternity.
All pain and suffering—left far behind, forever and forever.
If we could talk to the loved ones there now,
And get their story,
In the presence of Jesus and angels, rejoicing.
Its overwhelming—word's cannot describe.
Soon we'll all be together,
Living there with Jesus, and all the saints.
Then, when they roll the coffin into the sanctuary,
The time for grieving has begun, out of respect.
When it's my turn to leave,
If not the rapture
Then age eventually will take its toll.
I hope when people think about another one passing,
They'll just praise God.
Maybe God will allow me to come back,
Just to see,
Any who have gathered,
If we're not all gone
Even though they won't see me,
I pray for peace and celebration in their spirits,
Knowing it's more precious to be with Christ,
Than to remain on this earth,
Looking for His coming.

FACING THE FUTURE

IN THIS WORLD THERE'S JESUS

Much pain have I caused
    to see Jesus nailed to the tree,
All the sorrow He bore,
    bearing the curse to Calvary.
Now I'm living, always closer,
    each and every day,
To the home He's preparing,
    since He went away.

There are test's and trials,
    we may have to bear,
In each and every one,
    He'll always share.
Helping us along,
    every mile of the way,
Through the blood, the victory
    each and every day.

My life I give completely,
    to my Saviour and King,
All eternity with Him,
    who means everything.
All the cares of life
    no longer are mine,
Jesus carries them all,
    by His power divine.

This world may tremble,
    and the times grow dark,
Plans are in place—
    go with Jesus and embark.
If we're waiting and watching
    for that time to appear,
Jesus Christ will return,
    for His bride so dear.

GOD AND HIS SON

EVERYONE NEEDS JESUS

How the world needs Jesus,
Oh the love that He can give.
He's waiting now before you,
To see how you will live.

A wonderful peace He's giving,
With Him, day by day.
Jesus is all things,
Do you know Him today?

Jesus understands the problem,
Jesus Christ has the cure.
Turn to Jesus when faith is fallen,
Everything in Him is certain and sure.

I'm so glad I've found Jesus,
To feel His cleansing saving power.
On Calvary He bore all diseases.
We need Jesus, every hour.

FACING THE FUTURE

I'LL SERVE JESUS

I'm going to tell about Jesus,
Everywhere I go.
Going to shout aloud His praises,
Through this world below.

Since I met the Master,
He saved my sinful soul.
I want to tell the entire world,
That Jesus made me whole.

I'm going to walk with Jesus,
Hand in hand each day.
Going to depend on Him,
Every mile of the way.

Until that hour I shall see,
My Saviour face to face.
I'll keep trusting alone,
In Jesus saving grace.

Getting ready every day,
To make that special trip.
Holding to the lifeline,
Trusting I'll never slip.

As long as I put my life,
On the alter by grace,
I shall be safe and secure,
Till I see Him face to face.

GOD AND HIS SON

WALKING WITH JESUS

On this glorious way,
  I sometimes pause,
Still a man, I feel
  the burden of the cause.
So many are wandering,
  lost and alone,
Not serving Jesus,
  Who welcomes us home.

When I die I know,
  just where I'll go,
The Spirit lives in us—
  the saved really know.
In this temple of flesh,
  no longer we'll dwell,
Present with Jesus,
  in Heaven, not in Hell

Changed by the Spirit,
  God's power we know,
Live forever with Jesus—
  mortality can't go.
Rising through the skies,
  with the trumpet sound,
Forever with Jesus,
  on holy ground.

Have you asked God,
  what is holy?
Born again—
  the Bible tells us to be.
If God's Word speaks it,
  then it's so,
He lives inside us;
  to Heaven we will go.

FACING THE FUTURE

INTO THE FUTURE

The future is closing in, every single day,
We're in the Master plan, or gone astray.
Everyone must prepare—stay in tune,
The Creator of all is coming soon.

In this world, created in beauty,
Everything He made has its duty.
Even mankind, with a job in his hand:
Replentish, preserve the good of the land.

Everything going fine, then man fell,
One time in the garden—we know so well.
Forbidden to eat of a tree standing there,
Led all mankind down a road of despair.

Out of the garden, still not on His own,
Live and forgive, with God to atone.
Sacrifice needed—forgiveness from God,
An offering for pardon, while here on this sod.

Man's done it for ages, than God said, "Enough,"
A supreme sacrifice, help man from the rough.
Jesus, God's Son, was sent here to die,
To a cross at Calvary, from His home in the sky.

Than we must believe, and confess before God,
Be saved from the wrath, on this path we trod.
Try never to drift, too far from the shore,
Stay safe in His arms, free evermore.

GOD AND HIS SON

FACING THE FUTURE

We're facing the future every day,
Not knowing for sure, what will come our way.
Think about the path we travel on,
With faith to see each new day dawn.

Can't deny mistakes, made on the way,
Seek a foundation on which we can stay.
God's big sunshine, will light up our soul,
Jesus inside makes us whole.

Moving along this path through life,
We all are entwined in sin and strife.
Choose our steps with God's help, every day,
Our life on course—not going astray.

Seek for love, in our troubled world,
Have the flags of hope unfurled.
A lot depends on what we do every day,
Dear Jesus, help us, all along the way.

Tomorrows are in our Master's hands,
Man wants it all, in his own plans.
Peace is a blessing, to have if we try,
Home is in Heaven, in the sweet by and by.

Prophets prophesy about life's test,
All people must present, their very best.
The future keeps unfolding every day,
A New World is coming—Jesus way.

Don't fear wars—seek peace each day,
The Master heals this world's, vast decay.
Endure struggles, and dream all the way,
A new home is coming, all will be OK.

FACING THE FUTURE

GOD AND HIS SON

LOMAN BELLS CREATIONS

TO CONTACT=SEND $17.00 FOR A CD OR BOOK- or- $12.00 for a cassett, and your address to, loman bell, Murray River, rr#4, P.E,I, C0A1W0, Canada,Or e-mail =(lombell@yahoo.com) Or www.lomanharold bell.com. also some items aviable in stores now on the Island, also Itunes or amazone on the web

Hello my name is loman bell, welcome to my display of God given talents. Check some of them out.

www.ingramcontent.com/pod-product-compliance
Lightning Source LLC
Chambersburg PA
CBHW051211290426
44109CB00021B/2411